D0845329

THE CALIFORNIA TRAIL TO GOLD IN AMERICAN HISTORY

Other titles *in American History*

The Alamo
(ISBN 0-89490-770-0)

The Alaska Purchase
(ISBN 0-7660-1138-0)

Alcatraz Prison
(ISBN 0-89490-990-8)

The Battle of the Little Bighorn
(ISBN 0-89490-768-9)

The Boston Tea Party
(ISBN 0-7660-1139-9)

The California Gold Rush
(ISBN 0-89490-878-2)

The Chisholm Trail
(ISBN 0-7660-1345-6)

The Confederacy
and the Civil War
(ISBN 0-7660-1417-7)

The Fight for Women's
Right to Vote
(ISBN 0-89490-986-X)

The Great Depression
(ISBN 0-89490-881-2)

The Industrial Revolution
(ISBN 0-89490-985-1)

Japanese-American Internment
(ISBN 0-89490-767-0)

The Jim Crow Laws
and Racism
(ISBN 0-7660-1297-2)

John Brown's Raid
on Harpers Ferry
(ISBN 0-7660-1123-2)

Lewis and Clark's
Journey of Discovery
(ISBN 0-7660-1127-5)

The Lincoln Assassination
(ISBN 0-89490-886-3)

The Lindbergh Baby
Kidnapping
(ISBN 0-7660-1299-9)

The Louisiana Purchase
(ISBN 0-7660-1301-4)

The Manhattan Project
and the Atomic Bomb
(ISBN 0-89490-879-0)

McCarthy and the
Fear of Communism
(ISBN 0-89490-987-8)

The Mormon Trail
and the Latter-day Saints
(ISBN 0-89490-988-6)

Native Americans and
the Reservation
(ISBN 0-89490-769-7)

Nat Turner's Slave Rebellion
(ISBN 0-7660-1302-2)

The Oregon Trail
(ISBN 0-89490-771-9)

The Panama Canal
(ISBN 0-7660-1216-6)

Reconstruction Following
the Civil War
(ISBN 0-7660-1140-2)

The Salem Witchcraft Trials
(ISBN 0-7660-1125-9)

The Santa Fe Trail
(ISBN 0-7660-1348-0)

Shays' Rebellion and
the Constitution
(ISBN 0-7660-1418-5)

Slavery and Abolition
(ISBN 0-7660-1124-0)

The Transcontinental
Railroad
(ISBN 0-89490-882-0)

The Underground Railroad
(ISBN 0-89490-885-5)

The Union and the Civil War
(ISBN 0-7660-1416-9)

The Vietnam
Antiwar Movement
(ISBN 0-7660-1295-6)

The Watergate Scandal
(ISBN 0-89490-883-9)

IN
AMERICAN
HISTORY

THE CALIFORNIA TRAIL TO GOLD IN AMERICAN HISTORY

Carl R. Green

Enslow Publishers, Inc.
40 Industrial Road   PO Box 38
Box 398   Aldershot
Berkeley Heights, NJ 07922 Hants GU12 6BP
USA   UK
http://www.enslow.com

*This book is dedicated
to my intrepid grandchildren
Andrew, Becky, and Melissa Green
For them, the trail ahead holds nothing but promise.*

Library of Congress Cataloging-in-Publication Data

Green, Carl R.
The California trail to gold in American history / Carl R. Green.
p. cm. — (In American history)
Includes bibliographical references and index.
Summary: Examines the thrills and disappointments of the nineteenth-century rush for gold in California, during which people abandoned their jobs and homes and headed west in hopes of becoming rich.
ISBN 0-7660-1347-2
1. California—Gold discoveries Juvenile literature. 2. California Trail
Juvenile literature. 3. Voyages to the Pacific coast Juvenile literature.
[1. California—Gold discoveries. 2. California—History—1846–1850.]
I. Title. II. Series.
F865.G74 2000
979.4'04—dc21   99-37421
                                                         CIP

Printed in the United States of America

10 9 8 7 6 5 4 3 2 1

To Our Readers: All Internet addresses in this book were active and appropriate when we went to press. Any comments or suggestions can be sent by e-mail to Comments@enslow.com or to the address on the back cover.

★ CONTENTS ★

1

THE GOLDEN LURE

Back in the mid-1800s, Horace Greeley worked as editor of the *New York Tribune*. Like most Americans of the time, Greeley believed that pioneers would never be able to take wagons over the Rocky Mountains. In the *Tribune*, he wrote that only fools would try to trek overland to the West Coast. He changed his tune after settlers reported that they had found a route through the mountains to Oregon.

From that day on, Greeley took a new stance. Borrowing a phrase from a fellow newsman, he urged his readers to "Go west, young man." News of the gold strike in California added to his enthusiasm. In December 1848, he wrote, "We don't see any links . . . missing in the golden chain by which Hope is drawing her thousands of disciples to the new El Dorado, where fortune lies abroad upon the surface of the earth as plentiful as the mud in our streets."[1]

Spurred by dreams of easy riches, daring gold seekers prepared for the trek westward. Some took passage on ships headed out for the long voyage around South America. Others saved months of travel time by cutting

★ 7 ★

across the Isthmus of Panama. The most popular route, however, was the overland trail to the gold fields.

The first long leg of the journey to California followed the Oregon Trail. After crossing Wyoming's South Pass, California-bound travelers turned south. Ahead lay eight hundred miles of desert and mountain travel along the California Trail. With each cruel mile, these hardy men and women were building a nation that would truly stretch "from sea to shining sea."

An Epic Discovery

The year was 1848. The Mexican War was ending and the nation began to dream of settling its newly acquired territories. Dreaming was not the same as doing, however. Every mile that settlers traveled into the wilderness challenged their hearts and souls. California lay at the western edge of the continent, so remote that it seemed unreachable.

It took an epic discovery to hurry the westward movement. On January 24, 1848, James Marshall paused as he looked over the sawmill he was building on the American River in California. Something in the millrace that carried water to the mill wheel glinted in the sunlight. He later described the moment in these words: "My eye was caught by something shining in the bottom of the ditch. . . . I reached my hand down and picked it up; it made my heart thump, for I was certain it was gold. The piece was about half the size and shape of a pea. Then I saw another."[2]

Today, a replica of Sutter's Mill stands near the spot where James Marshall saw "something shining in the bottom of the ditch." The news that gold had been discovered in the American River spread quickly. Soon it seemed as though half the world was rushing to California to "strike it rich."

The small gold "peas" found at Sutter's Mill passed every test Marshall could devise. Jenny Wimmer, the camp cook, added a test of her own by dropping one of the nuggets into her soap kettle. When she fished it out of the boiling lye the nugget gleamed more brightly than ever. Marshall then reported the find to his boss, Capt. John Sutter. After the samples survived a bath of nitric acid, Sutter nodded in agreement. Marshall really had struck gold.

News of the Gold Strike Spreads

Sutter, who feared that gold seekers would overrun his land, tried to keep the news from spreading. He might as well have tried to hold back a river. Marshall's workers told their friends. The Wimmer boys shared the story with everyone they met. Sawmill workers showed off pouches filled with gold dust. *The Californian*, a San Francisco newspaper, soon picked up the story. The headline announced: "GOLD MINE FOUND."

Sam Brannan, the shopkeeper at Sutter's Fort, saw a chance to drum up trade. In May, he waved a bottle of gold dust in the air as he ran through the streets of San Francisco. "Gold! Gold! Gold from the American River!" Brannan shouted. The news spread quickly. Slowly at first, and then in a steady stream, men headed out to the gold fields.

Business in San Francisco slowed to a crawl. Shopkeepers closed their doors and carpenters laid down their tools. Farmers left their fields and sailors abandoned their ships. The army, which paid privates only six dollars a month, lost whole platoons of soldiers. Squads sent to arrest the deserters broke ranks and joined the fugitives in the gold fields. One soldier explained the fever in these words: "A frenzy seized my soul; piles of gold rose up before me at every step; thousands of slaves bowed to my beck and call; myriads of fair virgins contended for my love. In short I had a violent attack of gold fever."[3]

Sam Brannan stocked his store with shovels, tin pans, and picks. A spade that once cost a dollar now sold for ten dollars. The miners, blinded by dreams of golden treasure, shrugged and paid the inflated prices.

What was ten dollars to a man who would soon be rich? Every miner hoped to match the success of seven prospectors from Monterey. With American Indians doing the hard labor, the lucky seven and their workers unearthed 273 pounds of gold. After selling the gold for the standard sixteen dollars an ounce, the men pocketed $9,984 each. In 1848, when workers were lucky to earn a dollar a day, this was a fantastic fortune. Even greenhorns struck it rich. Not far from the new town of Sonora, a Los Angeles man picked a spot and started digging. Three feet down he struck a vein that yielded fifty-two pounds of gold.

The quiet waters of the American River once hid a king's ransom in gold. After its riches were exhausted, the Forty-Niners launched a search for new gold fields.

★ 11 ★

SOURCE DOCUMENT

GOLD MINE FOUND.—IN THE NEWLY MADE RACEWAY OF THE SAW MILL RECENTLY ERECTED BY CAPTAIN SUTTER, ON THE AMERICAN FORK, GOLD HAS BEEN FOUND IN CONSIDERABLE QUANTITIES. ONE PERSON BROUGHT THIRTY DOLLARS WORTH TO NEW HELVETIA, GATHERED THERE IN A SHORT TIME. CALIFORNIA, NO DOUBT, IS RICH IN MINERAL WEALTH; GREAT CHANCES HERE FOR SCIENTIFIC CAPITALISTS. GOLD HAS BEEN FOUND IN ALMOST EVERY PART OF THE COUNTRY.[4]

In the issue of March 15, 1848, The Californian devoted only a brief paragraph to the discovery that sparked the Gold Rush. It was not until May, when Sam Brannan ran through the streets shouting "Gold! Gold! Gold from the American River!" that gold fever struck San Francisco with stunning force.

For a time, the fever was confined to California. Easterners had heard rumors of gold strikes before, but none of them panned out. The doubts vanished after President James Polk spoke to Congress in December. Polk had been under fire for spending tax dollars on a "useless" war with Mexico. Now he saw a chance to defend his role in expanding the nation's borders. Polk began his speech by noting that California was known to possess valuable mines. "Recent discoveries," he said, "render it probable that these mines are more extensive and valuable than was anticipated." Then he dropped his bombshell. "The accounts of the abundance of gold in that territory," he told his listeners,

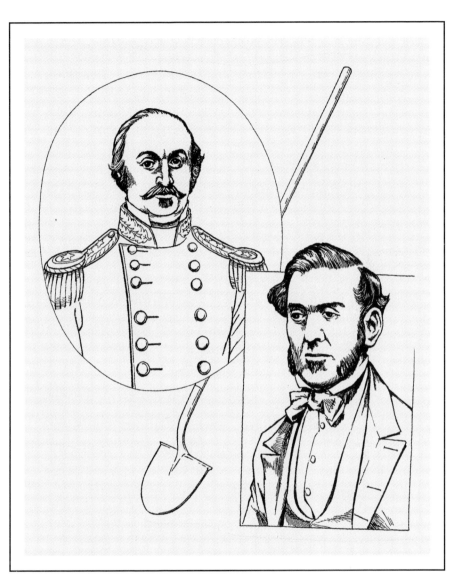

Captain John Sutter (left) owned the land on which James Marshall (right) made the discovery that set off the California Gold Rush. In the end, neither man profited from that historic moment in 1848. Sutter lost his battle with the hordes of gold seekers who overran his land, and Marshall was nearly penniless when he died.

"are of such an extraordinary character as would scarcely command belief were they not corroborated by authentic reports."[5] California's gold, Polk promised, would repay the costs of the war many times over.

An Attack of Gold Fever

Crowds gathered at the War Department to gawk at the 230 ounces of California gold displayed there. Polk's speech, backed up by the sight of the gold, started an epidemic. Gold fever raced along the East Coast, through the south, and into the Mississippi Valley. For the country, the news came at a good time. Money and credit were in short supply after the Panic of 1837. Wages had fallen as low as fifty cents a day. Farmers were feeling the pinch, too. Crop prices dipped and dipped again. Also, despite the hard times, Americans truly believed that their nation was destined to expand to the Pacific. The gold strike in California was seen as a just reward for the blood spilled in taking the land from Mexico.

Finally, with life growing more settled in the East, the frontier promised adventure. Americans from all walks of life prepared to test themselves against the wilderness. If they grew rich in the process, so much the better! For most gold seekers, the history of the land that drew them westward was of little concern.

★ THE FRONTIER IN AMERICAN HISTORY ★

The brave men and women who settled the American West did not think of themselves as the stuff of legends. They trekked westward hoping to find adventure, wealth, land, or perhaps a fresh start in life. Few stopped to think that the frontier was shaping them as surely as they were taming the wilderness.

In 1890, the federal government announced that the frontier no longer existed. The West, where the population had reached two or more persons per square mile, was declared settled. Historian Frederick Jackson Turner (1861–1932) seized on that turning point to discuss the importance of the frontier. "The existence of an area of free land, its continuous recession, and the advance of American settlement westward," he wrote, "explain American development."[6]

In Turner's view, the frontier changed the way Americans think and act. In the early days, he wrote, thousands of pioneers died in futile attempts to master the wilderness. Over time, new waves of pioneers reversed the process and brought the wilderness under control. In the process, whatever their ethnic background, the victors became "Americanized." This new species was restless, inventive, confident, and democratic. Matching wits with nature, Turner said, bred men and women who dreamed dreams and beheld visions.

Turner knew that Westerners could be as rude and greedy as their eastern cousins. Even so, he kept his faith in the goodness of the new American. The frontier, he pointed out, had served as a safety valve. When faced with failure, people went west and began again. Out there on the frontier, everyone started out equal. The weak gave up—or died. Success belonged to those who mastered that wild, bountiful land.

2

AN ISLAND CALLED CALIFORNIA

The Spanish sailors who sailed north from Mexico in the early 1500s had only myths to guide them. A popular novel of the day described California as an island ruled by Amazon women. Each woman, the writer declared, carried weapons made of gold and rode a griffin (a beast with the body of a lion and the head and wings of an eagle). The griffins, the novel warned, would devour any male who set foot on the island.

The truth was less fanciful. In 1542, Juan Rodríguez Cabrillo explored the California coastline as far north as Fort Ross. He found safe harbors and peaceful American Indians, but no Amazons, griffins, or gold. The Spanish, content for the moment with their conquest of Mexico, paid little heed to Cabrillo's discovery. That attitude changed after England's Sir Francis Drake dropped anchor in San Francisco Bay in 1579. The news meant that a hated rival had gained a foothold in California. Spain hurried to nail down its own claim.

SOURCE DOCUMENT

KNOW YE THAT ON HAND OF THE INDIES THERE IS AN ISLAND CALLED CALIFORNIA, VERY NEAR THE TERRESTRIAL PARADISE AND INHABITED BY BLACK WOMEN WITHOUT A SINGLE MAN AMONG THEM AND LIVING IN THE MANNER OF AMAZONS. THEY ARE ROBUST OF BODY, STRONG AND PASSIONATE IN HEART, AND OF GREAT VALOR. THEIR ISLAND IS ONE OF THE MOST RUGGED IN THE WORLD WITH BOLD ROCKS AND CRAGS. THEIR [WEAPONS] ARE ALL OF GOLD, AS IS THE HARNESS OF THE WILD BEASTS WHICH, AFTER TAMING, THEY RIDE. IN ALL THE ISLAND THERE IS NO OTHER METAL.[1]

California and its gold first caught the imagination of Europeans in the early 1500s. The novel Las Sergas de Esplandián *created the myth that California was an island ruled by an immensely rich Amazon queen called Calafía. Later explorations found tribes of American Indians, but failed to find the fabled Amazon women. In 1747, King Ferdinand VI of Spain laid the second half of the myth to rest. "California," he proclaimed, "is not an island."*

Spanish California

Sebastián Vizcaíno set the stage in 1602 by charting the coastline. Wars in Europe and troubles in her colonies, however, slowed the Spanish march northward from Mexico. In the end the task of colonizing California fell to the Catholic Church. The Spanish crown made the church aware of its desire to found colonies and bring Christianity to the local American Indians. As a result, the church perfected the mission system. Father Eusebio Kino began by building a chain of twenty-nine mission churches in Mexico. In 1769, his successors marched north to continue the work.

By the time the padres (priests) were finished, twenty-one missions stretched from San Diego to Sonoma. Father Junípero Serra founded nine of them. Located roughly a day's ride apart, the missions lay along a trail called El Camino Real (the King's Highway). Once a mission site was chosen, the padres baptized the local American Indians and quickly put them to work. Those converts who settled down to work in the mission's fields and workshops gave up their traditional way of life. In return, the priests provided food, shelter, and instruction in Catholic beliefs and practices. Thanks to the climate, the fertile soil, and the hard work of the new Christians, the missions flourished. Fields of wheat, corn, beans, and grapes produced bumper crops. Herds of cattle, horses, and sheep roamed the grasslands.

The Spanish, as well as the gold seekers who came later, misjudged the American Indians they found in California. Because the coastal tribes were not as technologically advanced as the Aztecs or the Plains tribes, the invaders scorned them as "diggers." Closer study later proved that the native people were neither lazy nor backward. If they seemed idle to the whites, it was because food and shelter came easily. Although the newcomers scorned most American Indians as "dirty," it was the newcomers who needed lessons in hygiene. Tribal members scraped themselves clean in sweathouses and kept their camps clean by moving

Blessed with a mild climate and an abundant food supply, California's American Indian tribes lived simple, mostly peaceful lives. For shelter, they built thatched wickiups known as kiitcha each time they moved to a new campsite. These reconstructed kiitcha stand on a quiet hillside above San Diego's Old Town.

them frequently. In church on Sundays, Catholic priests often accused their new converts of lax moral conduct. In truth, the native Californians learned many of their vices (drunkenness, for example) from white men.

Spain sent two types of settlers north from Mexico. One group was poorly prepared for frontier life. Some were criminals. Others drowned themselves in drink and idleness. The second group was made up of settlers whose families belonged to Spain's ruling class. California's governors paid off favors by granting large tracts of land known as *ranchos* to these well-born newcomers.

The fast-growing ranchos, coupled with the missions, gave Spanish California its distinctive way of life. Like the mission priests, the *rancheros* (ranch owners) put American Indians to work in their fields and pastures. The prosperous ranchos supported the rancheros in a gracious lifestyle filled with fine horses and frequent *fiestas* (parties).

Mexican Rule Ends the Reign of the Missions

In 1821, the people of Mexico threw out their Spanish rulers and declared their independence. The new government, beset by problems at home, ignored its remote provinces. Left largely to its own affairs, California drifted. The north feuded with the south, and the rancheros feuded with the mission priests. California's American Indians, weary of forced labor, rose in revolt at several missions in 1824. Mexican troops crushed the uprisings, but mission life was never the same.

Laws passed in Mexico City transferred control of mission lands to local officials. These officials, in turn, gave the rich fields to the American Indians who worked them. The new owners, however, were ill prepared to protect their property rights. Some sold their land for whiskey and trinkets. Others simply drifted away. By the late 1830s the "mission Indian" population had fallen from some thirty thousand to less than four thousand. Wealthy rancheros gobbled up some eight million acres and put the remaining American Indians to work. Unlike the mission priests, the new foremen treated servants and field hands like serfs. Instead of pay, the workers received only food, clothing, and a place to sleep.

Cattle grazed and multiplied on the lush grasslands. The herds roamed free for much of the year, unhampered by fences. At roundup time, *vaqueros* (cowboys) cut their rancho's cattle out of the herds and slaughtered those earmarked for market. The profit lay mainly in by-products. Workers boiled the fat in iron kettles to make tallow. Half a world away, Boston factories used the tallow to make candles, soap, and lubricants. The hides, so precious that they were known as "California bank notes," were staked out in the sun to dry. Later, after workers scraped and salted the hides, the rancheros sold them to Yankee and Mexican sea captains. As many as eighty thousand hides a year changed hands, at prices ranging from $1.50 to $2.50 a hide. The income paid for the fine clothes, tools, saddles, and wine the frontier province did not produce.[2]

Profit-hungry American traders often failed to see the beauty of the ranchero lifestyle. One thrifty Yankee, Richard Henry Dana, described his impressions of California in *Two Years Before the Mast* (1840). The rancheros' lavish spending, he wrote, shocked him:

> The Californians are an idle, thriftless people, and can make nothing for themselves. The country abounds in grapes, yet they buy bad wine made in Boston and

brought round by us, at an immense price, and retail it among themselves at a *real* [twelve and a half cents] by the small wineglass. Their hides too, which they value at two dollars in money, they give for something which costs seventy-five cents in Boston; and buy shoes (as like as not, made of their own hides, which have been carried twice round Cape Horn) at three and four dollars, and "chicken-skin boots" at fifteen dollars apiece. Things sell on an average at an advance of nearly three hundred per cent upon the Boston prices.[3]

Dana's fellow Americans did grasp two facts. First, California was an untapped treasure chest. The land was fertile, the climate mild—and small amounts of gold were found near Los Angeles in 1842. Second, Mexico's

California's Spanish settlers failed to find the Amazon women described by legend, but they did find a mild climate and fruitful soil. Before long, the missions and ranchos were grazing cattle on the hillsides and growing grapes in the valleys.

hold on its distant province was feeble at best. California was ripe for the taking—if an overland route could be opened across two thousand miles of wilderness.

The United States Faces Westward

In 1803, President Thomas Jefferson made one of history's best bargains—the Louisiana Purchase. For 15 million dollars, France sold all of the land between the Mississippi River and the Rocky Mountains. Jefferson then dispatched Captains Meriwether Lewis and William Clark to explore this vast region. Aided by Sacagawea, an American Indian woman originally of the Shoshone tribe, the expedition reached the coast of Oregon in 1805. The reports published by Lewis and Clark helped convince the young nation that its destiny lay westward.

In the years that followed, more and more Americans found their way to California. Whalers and traders made the long voyage around stormy Cape Horn at the southern tip of South America. As one Spanish official noted, "The Anglo-Americans . . . come with arrogant boldness to anchor in our very harbors, and to act with the same liberty as if they were Spanish." The official warned that "this proud nation, . . . may one day venture to measure [its strength] with Spain, and acquiring such knowledge of our seas and coasts may make California the object of its attack."[4]

By the 1820s fearless mountain men were threading their way through the wilderness in search of furs. For a time they were content to set their traps in the mountains. That changed in 1826 when Jedediah Smith led a party from Utah to the San Gabriel mission near Los Angeles. The epic journey took sixty exhausting days.

The padres welcomed Smith and his ragged band, but Mexican officials viewed the Americans with suspicion. After some wary bargaining the governor forgave the trespass, but asked Smith to return to Utah by the same southern route. Smith agreed—and promptly broke his word. Instead of turning south, he headed east across the Sierras. Bogged down in deep snow, the party was forced to hole up in a snug valley camp. Smith and two friends rested for a time and then tried again. This time the three men managed to push through the mountains and made it back to their base in Utah. The road to California was steep and treacherous—but now it lay open.

New pathfinders stepped forward. One was mountain man Joseph Walker. In 1833, Walker crossed the Sierras east to west over the pass that now bears his name. The exhausting journey at last led the party into the splendid Yosemite Valley. There the men gazed in awe at the great trees that came to be known as Giant Sequoias. A few years later, Walker led a wagon train westward over the route he had blazed. That route would soon become a major segment of the California Trail.

Mexican War and a Change of Flag

Back in Washington, D.C., interest in California was growing. U.S. leaders feared that the region's weak defenses would invite an attack by Great Britain or

The rigors of winter in the Sierra Nevada mountains are shown clearly in this 1841 engraving of explorer John C. Frémont's campsite. In their eagerness to reach California, many gold seekers ignored the dangers and perished along the trail.

France. President Andrew Jackson tried to buy California in the early 1830s, but his envoy bungled the deal. In 1842, fearing that war with Britain was near, an American naval officer seized Monterey and hauled down the Mexican flag. When British warships failed to appear, the officer said he was sorry and withdrew.

In June 1846, a handful of settlers took matters into their own hands. An "army" of thirty-three American hotheads captured Sonoma and raised the flag of a new republic. A wealthy ranchero later wrote that the flag's central symbol "was so badly painted . . . that it looked more like a pig than a bear."[5] The Bear Flag Republic lasted until July 7, when Commodore

John Sloat raised the Stars and Stripes over Monterey. By this time the United States and Mexico were engaged in a full-scale war.

For the most part, California was a sideshow during the Mexican War. The struggle focused mainly on Texas, which the United States had annexed in 1845. When diplomats failed to settle the conflict, Congress declared war on May 13, 1846. Even though American troops won victories in northern Mexico, the war dragged on. In the end, U.S. forces landed at Veracruz (a port on the Gulf of Mexico) and fought their way into Mexico City.

Spain brought Christianity to California in the form of a chain of twenty-one mission churches. In central California, the mission at San Juan Bautista (shown here) still stands.

At the same time, American forces in California were winning further victories. One small, determined unit drove south and occupied Los Angeles. Afterward, instead of dealing fairly with the proud rancheros, Captain Archibald Gillespie tried to intimidate them. The harsh treatment sparked a ranchero uprising that drove the tiny American army out of the city. In December 1846 the superb horsemen defeated General Stephen Kearny's newly arrived troops in the Battle of San Pascual. The Americans regrouped and launched a new attack that drove their foes out of Los Angeles. By this time the rancheros knew they were outnumbered and outgunned. Andres Pico signed the papers on January 13, 1847, that ended Mexican control of California.

The defeats at home and in California brought the Mexican government to the peace table. Early in 1848, the Treaty of Guadalupe Hidalgo awarded the entire Southwest to the United States. The stage was set for the California Gold Rush.

★ A CALIFORNIA FIESTA ★

The first American visitors to California were quick to criticize the Spanish settlers. Those who opened their hearts to the graceful lifestyle of the rancheros soon changed their tune.

The highlight of life on the ranchos was the fiesta. Major fiestas celebrated roundups, weddings, births, and other events. When the great day arrived, guests rode in from miles around. The men adorned their horses with plumes and braided ribbons into the horses' tails and manes. Then they vaulted into silver-inlaid saddles and showed off their riding skills. Other amusements included racing, bullfighting, and bear baiting. In the evening everyone gathered for a dance party known as a *fandango*.

Richard Henry Dana attended a wedding fandango in Santa Barbara. A hundred or more guests crowded into a tent set up by the bride's father. The older women clapped in time to violin and guitar music. The younger women danced sedately in their long, lacy dresses. Dana admired the women, but thought the men danced with more grace and spirit.

Earlier in the day, the women had filled empty eggshells with confetti or cologne. Now, as the evening wore on, they put their fragile missiles to work. The trick was to slip up behind a man and knock his hat aside. Then, with a swift movement, the woman smashed the eggshell on her victim's head and ducked out of sight. The man, with cologne streaming down his face, spun around and looked for his attacker. Unless the woman wanted to be caught, he would see only a row of smiling faces.

A second game gave the young men a chance to do some courting. While the young women were dancing, a man would sneak up and place his hat on a girl's head. That was a signal for her to toss the hat to the floor—or to go on dancing. If she left the hat in place, this meant that she welcomed its owner as her companion for the evening.

Dana says that the fandango went on for three days and nights. His host asked him to perform an American dance, but he declined. "After [I saw] the ridiculous figure some of our countrymen cut in dancing [compared to] the Mexicans," he wrote, "we thought it best to leave it to their imaginations."[6]

3

GOLD FEVER STRIKES

All through the spring of 1848 San Francisco's *Californian* tracked the story of the gold strike at Sutter's Mill. Was the news for real? The first stories were full of doubts. Later reports, however, assured readers that the gold was both real and plentiful. Then, on May 29, the newspaper announced that it was closing down. The editor explained, "The whole country, from San Francisco to Los Angeles, and from the sea shore to the base of the Sierra Nevadas, resounds with the sordid cry of '*gold*, GOLD, GOLD!' . . . [T]he field is left half planted, the house half built, and everything neglected but the manufacture of shovels and pickaxes."[1]

Hopes ran high as the Gold Rush gained speed. No one seemed to know how best to do the mining, but all agreed that the gold was there for the taking. For the most part, gold seekers worried more about how to transport their treasure than how to find it. Some put their faith in iron strongboxes. Others said they would make do with leather bags. The fever did have its limits. One miner declared, "If I don't pick up

★ 29 ★

more than a hatful of gold a day, I shall be perfectly satisfied."[2]

Gold fever swept the eastern half of the nation with equal force. On December 6, 1848, the *Daily Courant* of Hartford, Connecticut, cautioned its readers, "The California gold fever is approaching its crisis. . . . Thither is now setting a tide that will not cease its flow until either untold wealth is amassed, or extended beggary is secured. . . . Fifteen millions have already come into the possession of somebody, and all creation is going out there to fill their pockets with the great condiment of their diseased minds."[3]

Why did a soft yellow metal inspire such frenzy? The answer lies in the human desire to possess objects that are either rare or beautiful. Gold meets the test on both counts. First, the supply is severely limited, which makes it ideal for coining money. Second, gold can be shaped into lovely, durable objects such as jewelry. The fact that gold's only practical use in 1848 was in making false teeth did not lower its value. Lucky prospectors could—and did—become rich overnight.

Who Were the Gold Seekers?

In May 1848 the prospectors working the gold fields could be counted in the hundreds. By the end of the year the number had mushroomed to at least ten thousand. Some of these early birds picked up their treasure and hurried to turn it into cash. The sight of so many buckskin bags filled with gold silenced the last few doubters.

The *New York Herald* reported the arrival of gold fever in the city. Two-thirds of all New Yorkers, the paper noted, were either leaving for California or planning to do so. A Scotsman who observed the Gold Rush later wrote, "Among the Americans en route for California were men of all classes—professional men, merchants, labourers, sailors, farmers, mechanics, and numbers of long, gaunt Western men, with rifles as long as themselves."[4] One Michigan group was made up of farmers, clerks, blacksmiths, doctors, lawyers, and preachers.

The bold message painted on this covered wagon sums up the feverish spirit of the Gold Rush. As the news spread, farmers left their fields, clerks tossed aside their pens, and soldiers deserted their units. The entire nation seemed caught up in the cries of "Gold, Gold, Gold!"

Anyone who claimed to be an expert on California or on gold mining was in demand. Geology professors polished their lectures and spoke to eager crowds. Their talks covered topics such as finding, testing, and washing gold. Shops sold out of any book that promised to guide the reader to the gold fields. The best of the lot was Edwin Bryant's *What I Saw in California*, which hit the market in 1848. Unlike some of his fellow authors, Bryant had seen the places he described. Readers were hypnotized by passages such as this word picture of a mirage:

> In the course of the morning, I noticed [a] mirage in great perfection. A wide cascade . . . of glittering, foaming, and tumbling waters was . . . perfectly well defined on the slope of the mountains to our left. . . . Below this was a limpid lake, so calm and mirror-like that it reflected with all the distinctness of reality the tall, inverted shapes of the mountains and all the scenery beyond its . . . illusory surface. Nature, in this desert region, if she does not furnish the reality, frequently presents the ghosts of beautiful objects and scenery.[5]

As 1849 dawned, the gold bug raced through cities, towns, and across the countryside. The year gave the hordes of gold seekers their nickname—the Forty-Niners. Out near Youngstown, New York, the fever hit farmer William Swain. Swain, like many young men, yearned for adventure as well as for riches. As the fever grew, he discussed his plans with his wife, Sabrina, and his brother, George. Sabrina, nursing a new baby, begged him not to go. George took his brother's side. He agreed to work the farm while William was gone.

Swain and three friends started for Buffalo on April 11, 1849. In his diary, the young Forty-Niner described the pain of saying good-bye. "I parted from my family completely unable to restrain my emotions and left them all bathed in tears," he wrote, "even my brother, whose energy of mind I never saw fail before."[6]

Preparing for the Journey

Making the decision to "get rich quick" in the gold fields was easy. Finding money to finance the trip

SOURCE DOCUMENT

HO FOR CALIFORNIA.—FOR SALE CHEAP, THE WELL KNOWN PUBLIC HOUSE ALANTHUS, NOW KEPT BY FRANCIS O. SPEIGHT. REASON FOR SELLING, HE IS GOING TO CALIFORNIA. INQUIRE ON THE PREMISES, CORNER OF WAVERLY PLACE AND McDOUGAL STREET.

FOR CALIFORNIA.—$1,000 WANTED BY A PERSON GOING TO CALIFORNIA, FOR WHICH ONE HALF THE ENTIRE PROCEEDS OF HIS LABOR FOR TWO YEARS WILL BE GIVEN, OR THE SAME FOR ONE YEAR FOR ONE HALF THE ABOVE AMOUNT. REFERENCE AND SECURITY GIVEN. ADDRESS T.C.E., BROADWAY POST OFFICE.[7]

Francis Speight and T.C.E. placed these ads in the New York Herald *in December 1848 and January 1849. As gold fever spread, the cost of heading off to California forced gold seekers to extreme measures. Some, who could not borrow or beg the money, sold their property or offered to indenture themselves. Speight most likely did sell his public house (probably an inn or a tavern), and it is likely that T.C.E. found a backer.*

was tougher. A lucky few had savings to draw on or property to sell. Most of the gold seekers, however, traveled on borrowed funds. William Swain declared himself ready to leave after he raised $250. With money in hand, the gold seekers next had to outfit themselves.

The newspapers ran ads for gear that ranged from bowie knives to folding rubber boats. Clothing stores stocked woolen shirts, flannel longjohns, baggy jeans, felt hats, and high-top boots. A few travelers showed how little they knew about the gold country by packing formal evening wear. Enos Christman was one of those who overdid the packing. Young Christman stuffed his trunk with seventeen pairs of pants, thirty-five shirts, seven coats, and five waistcoats. Women rushed to prepare sewing kits called "bachelors' companions" for their fathers, husbands, and boyfriends.[8] The men agreed they would need the needles and thread to mend what they could not replace.

Only the most reckless Forty-Niners planned to live off the land. Travelers stocked up on flour, bacon, hard biscuits, lard, sugar, and corn meal. Those who could afford a luxury or two packed jars of pickles, candied fruit, and jugs of brandy. To treat disease and wounds, the emigrants added healing lotions, purgatives, sulfur, and other medicines. Anxious wives and mothers tossed in patent remedies such as Gay's California Cachalangua. The label carried this legend: *"For what is wealth compared with health?"*

Hunger and disease were not the only dangers that lay ahead. To fight off raiders and bandits, the gold

THE CALIFORNIA TRAIL
1841–59

*Independence, Missouri to
Sutter's Fort, California*

The trail from Missouri to California crossed two thousand miles of wilderness. Until the caravans crossed the Continental Divide at South Pass, families bound for Oregon and California followed the same route. Once they reached the Parting of the Ways, the Forty-Niners had two routes from which to pick.

seekers armed themselves with pistols, rifles, knives, sword canes, and even blackjacks (a leather-covered hand weapon). The weapons did not come cheap. William Swain paid fourteen dollars for a revolver and powder flask (about $350 in today's money). A friend shelled out eighteen dollars for a double-barreled shotgun. Out on the prairie, an army officer watched columns of armed men sweep past and shook his head. "Arms of all kinds must certainly be scarce in the States," he remarked, "after such a drain as the emigrants have made upon them."[9]

Which Route Should We Take?

Many Forty-Niners joined companies of fellow gold seekers. In Massachusetts, over a hundred companies set out for California in 1849. Some groups were small, but others enrolled a hundred men or more. All made careful plans and drilled members in their duties. William Swain and his friends signed on with a Michigan group called the Wolverine Rangers. Each Ranger chipped in one hundred dollars and agreed to share expenses, supplies, and (if all went well) profits.

Sooner or later, each company turned to the problem of picking a route. One choice carried gold seekers by boat around Cape Horn, at the tip of South America. Newspapers dubbed these seafarers the Argonauts. The name was drawn from the myth of the Greek hero Jason, who sailed on the *Argo* in search of the Golden Fleece. Many Easterners chose this route, even though they knew it meant spending up to eight months at sea.

In 1850, a speedy clipper ship called the *Sea Witch* cut that time to a record ninety-seven days.[10] Fast or slow, the gold seekers reached the gold fields worn down by bad food, cramped quarters, and months of boredom.

To save time, some Argonauts spent four hundred dollars for a ticket on a sea-and-land route. The first leg of the five-week journey took them to Central America and Panama's port of Chagres. From Chagres the travelers crossed the Isthmus of Panama by canoe and by mule. The journey to the Pacific coast was a four-day marathon of heat, mud, mosquitoes, and jungle fevers. Even then, the ordeal was not over. Weeks might pass before a ship arrived to carry the eager gold seekers north to California. A few hardy Argonauts avoided Panama by crossing Mexico on horseback. Once they reached the Pacific, they booked passage on a ship headed north.

Overland on the California Trail

The most popular route led Forty-Niners overland on the Oregon-California Trail. This cheaper, quicker journey cut nearly fourteen thousand miles off the voyage around Cape Horn. The first leg brought the emigrants by rail, riverboat, and horseback to Missouri. At St. Joseph and other jumping-off points, they joined wagon trains and headed west. Some twelve hundred miles of hard going took them to Wyoming's South Pass. Soon afterward they said farewell to friends bound for Oregon and turned south toward California. Ahead lay eight hundred miles of desert heat and mountain cold. Alert wagon masters

SOURCE DOCUMENT

LANCASTER OHIO
OCTOBER 18TH, 1852

MY DEAR HUSBAND,

I RECIVED YOUR KIND LETTER WHICH FOUND US ENJOYING GOOD HEALTH. I WAS GLAD TO HEARE THAT YOU . . . HAVE ARIVED THERE SAFE, YOU WAS NO LONGER ON THE ROAD THAN I EXPECTED YOU WOULD BE, BUT I AM GLAD THAT YOU GOT THROUGH SAFE. . . .

I WOULD LIKE TO HAVE YOU HOME FOR I AM VERY LONELY WITHOUT YOU. PROVISIONS ARE HIGH HERE, . . . THEY ARE SELLING AT CITY PRICES. MY PIGS ARE FINE ORDER, I MUST BUY SOME MORE CORN THIS WEEK, THEY COST ME GREAT DEAL. . . . WE CANNOT GET ANY ONE TO SAW YOUR WOOD HALF THE TIME & IT COST SO MUCH. WE HAVE A GOOD GARDEN THIS SUMMER, CABBAGE FIRST RATE, SWEET POTATOES VERY FINE. . . .

I AM SO LONESOME, TIRED & DISCOURAGED & EVERYTHING. I SUPPOSE THAT YOU DO YOUR WASHING YOURSELF. I HAVE HAD ONE TOOTH DRAWN SINCE YOU LEFT BUT MY HEALTH OTHER WISE HAS BEEN VERY GOOD. . . .

YOU MUST NOT FAIL TO WRITE ME WHEN YOU GET THIS, YOU MUST EXCUSE BAD WRITING AS I HAVE BEEN WASHING ALL DAY & MY HANDS IS STIFF. I MUST NOW CLOSE MY LETER FOR IT IS DARK AND I MUST SEND IT TO THE OFFICE. . . .

I REMAIN YOUR AFFECTIONATE WIFE. WRITE SOON.[11]

David and Rachel Ann Brown were African Americans who lived in the free state of Ohio. Like many wives who watched their husbands head off to California, Rachel stayed home and struggled to make ends meet. In the evenings she wrote letters to her "dear husband." She wrote this letter of her troubles after learning that David had arrived safely in California. As time passed, however, her hopes for a brighter future faded. David bought a house and settled in California—but never sent for his faithful Rachel.

kept a wary eye on the calendar. They knew that early winter snows could close down the passes through the Sierra Nevada Mountains. Less popular was a longer southern trail that avoided the worst of the mountain barrier. This route followed the Santa Fe Trail to New Mexico before veering west to California.

The wear and tear of the overland journey took its toll on men, women, and children. Judge Eleazer Ingalls noted that fact in this diary entry headed "Humboldt Desert, July 28, 1850:"

> The appearance of the emigrants has sadly changed since we started. Then they were full of life . . . and the road was enlivened with the song of "I am going to California with my tin pan on my knee." . . . [B]ut now they crawl along hungry and spiritless, and if a song is raised at all, it is, "Oh carry me back to Old Virginia, to Old Virginia's shore."[12]

Mountain men like Jedediah Smith took the long, hard days in stride. Most Forty-Niners were new to the frontier and its hardships. Many had never traveled farther than twenty miles from home. Life on the trail taught them about backbreaking work, hunger, thirst, sickness, fear, and death. A few turned back, but most trudged on toward the land of their golden dreams.

★ TRAVEL BY AERIAL NAVIGATION ★

Gold, the Forty-Niners told themselves, would be easy to find once they reached California. In their minds, getting there was the major challenge. Whether the gold seeker traveled by ship or by wagon, the journey was measured in weeks and months. The urge to cut that travel time inspired some truly off-the-wall thinking.

A few hopefuls put their faith in the wind-wagon. To onlookers, the vehicle appeared to be a cross between a sailboat and a wagon. The first model hit fifteen miles per hour as the wind filled the sails and drove the wagon forward. Moments later, the hybrid craft veered out of control and crashed. The builder, "Wind-wagon" Thomas, never found a way to fix the flaws in his design.

Rufus Porter, editor of *Scientific American* magazine, thought he had a better idea. Why not fly to California? A pamphlet titled "Aerial Navigation: The Practicability of Traveling Pleasantly and Safely from New York to California in Three Days" spelled out the scheme. Passengers, Porter promised, would gaze at wild horses and grizzly bears as they cruised above prairies and mountains.

The Aerial Locomotive was first cousin to a modern blimp. The plans showed a passenger cabin that hung beneath a huge hydrogen-filled gas bag. The bag itself was to be made of spruce rods covered with arrow-proof cloth. Powerful steam engines, Porter said, would speed three hundred passengers westward at a hundred miles an hour. If a storm approached, the pilot would steer safely above the danger.

Porter then turned to the thorny issue of costs. His estimates showed that the Aerial Locomotive could be built for $1,750. Leaving off the engines, he added in a puzzling note, would reduce the cost to under a thousand

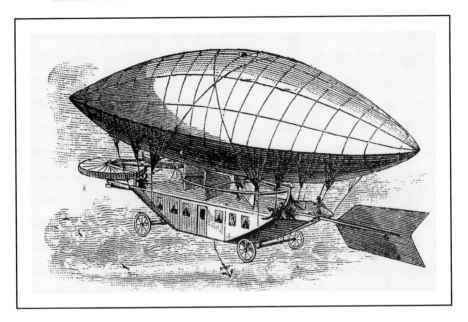

Rather than face the ordeal of travel by land or by sea, a few hopeful gold seekers put their faith in the Aerial Locomotive. Rufus Porter promised his steam-powered blimp would fly three hundred passengers to California in as little as three days. The airship, however, flew only in Porter's fertile imagination.

dollars. Porter next turned to the matter of ticket prices. To drum up business for the first trip he offered three hundred tickets at a cut-rate price of fifty dollars each. Later trips, he said, would cost two hundred dollars.

Porter's sales pitch pulled in orders for some two hundred tickets. The wonderful Locomotive, however, never left the drawing board. Most likely, engineers stepped forward to point out its flaws. Given the massive weight of the airship, it could never have lifted from the ground.[13]

4

THE LONG WAY AROUND

The year 1848 was drawing to a close. Americans young and old were talking about gold and how they would gather their share of the wealth that lay waiting in California. An ad for a trip to California that ran in the *New York Herald* on December 29 was a sign of the times:

CALIFORNIA—FOR SAN FRANCISCO DIRECT— A first class ocean Steamship, of 1,800 tons burthen, will be dispatched for the above port early in the month of February, should a sufficient number of passengers offer to make it an object. This will be undoubtedly the best possible way of reaching the Gold mines in the shortest time—avoiding all contingencies which are feared may happen on other routes. The steamship has unsurpassed accommodations for passengers, both in cabins and steerage. Her machinery has been well tested, and can be relied upon; and as a sea craft, she has no superior. For passage apply to

J. HOWARD & SON, 73 South street.[1]

J. Howard & Son probably were swamped with requests for passage on the steamer. For the most part, easterners preferred a long sea voyage to the more direct overland route. Most knew more about ships than they did about mule teams and wagons. Perhaps they also felt safer riding out a storm at sea than risking the loss of their scalps to Sioux or Pawnee raiders.

Some Argonauts sailed alone and on the spur of the moment. Most reined in their impatience and joined a group of fellow gold seekers. The Boston & California Joint Mining & Trading Company chartered a ship named the *Edward Everett* and sailed in January 1849. Its well-to-do members included students, craftsmen, merchants, eight sea captains, four doctors, and a geologist. To keep spirits high the leaders planned band concerts, Sunday church services, and midweek prayer meetings. The geologist lectured on mining techniques. Packed away in the cargo hold were mining tools, steam engines, and enough lumber to build two houses. Food stocks took up a fair share of the cargo space. The *Everett* carried 250 barrels of flour and fifty thousand pounds of bread—but "not an item of spirituous liquors." Given that claim, how did the leaders explain the twenty-five gallons of whiskey that found its way aboard? The whiskey, they said, was for "medicinal purposes."[2]

Less wealthy Argonauts relied on their powers of invention. William Neil handed a "promise to pay" signed by his brother to a ship's agent. To sweeten the deal he also offered to insure his life for two thousand dollars. "If I die," he said, "then you may deduct the [ticket price] of $250, and pay the balance over to my brother." In New York, eight young men volunteered to serve as rowers on a sailing ship. As they explained it, there surely would be days when the winds died and left the ship becalmed. At that point they vowed to keep the ship moving by towing it behind their small rowboat. The agent told them they were out of their minds.[3]

Men outnumbered women on these voyages ten to one. Most of the women who did make the trip traveled with their husbands or parents. The sight of a

The stormy, icy seas around Cape Horn spelled disaster for many ships. This leg of the perilous journey gave Argonauts ample reason to regret the day they embarked on the long voyage.

woman traveling alone was rare enough to excite comment. "Charlie," the newspaper *Alta California* reported, displayed "a brace of pistols and a dazzling bowie knife, [and] defied insult." Her mission, she declared, was "to pursue and demolish a traitorous escort, who had robbed and deserted her at New Orleans." Whatever her resolve, Charlie's quest had a happy ending. When she reached San Francisco, a young man met her ship and clasped Charlie in his arms. Charlie, it turned out, had a forgiving nature.[4]

Hazards of Long Months at Sea

The Argonauts who sailed around Cape Horn knew they would be at sea for six to eight months. After the thrill of departure wore off, each day began to look the same as the one before. To fight boredom the passengers played cards, read books, put on plays, cleaned their weapons, and wrote in their journals. A practical joke or two sometimes eased the tension, as did the sport of albatross "fishing." Men caught the huge birds by dragging a baited hook behind the ship. When an albatross pecked at the lure, the hook caught in its beak. The "fishermen" then pulled in their catch. George Dornin measured one albatross at ten feet six inches, wingtip to wingtip.[5]

Boredom sapped the spirits of the Argonauts, but illness took their lives. The landlubbers' first taste of woe came when seasickness struck. Lying on deck with their heads hung over the side, passengers felt certain they would die. One "cure" was to drink seawater. The treatment touched off a bout of violent retching, but most victims felt better by the next day. The misery of seasickness was only a taste of what lay ahead. Diets lacking in the vitamin C found in fresh fruits and vegetables caused a disease called scurvy. Victims first felt weak, then broke out in sores. Their joints became swollen and their gums turned spongy. When left untreated, the disease was almost always fatal. If cholera struck a ship, the end came faster. The dreaded disease sometimes killed a quarter of the crew and passengers in a few days.

Even on the best of ships, the food was hard to stomach. Hiram Pierce described the breakfast menu on the run up to San Francisco as "coffey, hard bread and molasses." The main meal of the day came at noon and consisted of "pork, corned beef & beans or rice sometimes." For supper, he ate "bread and sugar. Butter is served," he added, "but the sight is sufficient without the smell."[6] Richard Henry Dana complained that for weeks at a time the sailors ate nothing but salt beef and salt pork. On Christmas the cook served a plum pudding—but held back the usual ration of molasses. Dana wrote that the loss of their favorite treat left the crew in a bad mood.[7]

Foul weather was another danger that awaited the Argonauts. Storms could strike at any time, but the roughest waters raged around Cape Horn. Scores of ships sank under the onslaught of the cape's fierce winds and towering waves. Elizabeth Gunn survived to describe one terrible storm:

A gale commenced on Tuesday at noon and lasted till Friday, and we were tossed about in fine order. . . . We could not go to the table. The children sat against the side of the cabin, and held their plates in their laps, and half the time one would spill his water or lose his spoon. . . . And you can no more walk . . . than you can fly. Down, down you slide till you land against the wall, and there you are fast at last and must try it over again.[8]

In 1850, Mrs. D. B. Bates went through a far greater ordeal when she sailed for San Francisco with her husband, who was the ship's captain. During a

Forty-Niners who took the shortcut across the Isthmus of Panama sailed up the Chagres River by canoe. The sights and sounds of the jungle delighted adventurous gold seekers. Others fretted about the heat, the alligators, and the risk of contracting yellow fever.

storm in the Atlantic Ocean, the ship's cargo of coal caught fire. The cabins filled with smoke, and Mrs. Bates was forced to spend five days on deck while the storm raged around her. The *Nonantum* limped on to the Falkland Islands (located slightly northeast of Cape Horn), where Captain Bates scuttled (purposely sank) the ship. A second coal ship picked them up—and it, too, caught fire. After drifting for a time in a lifeboat, the Bateses were rescued by a passing ship. From there they transferred to a fourth ship, the *Fanchon*—which also carried coal. Three days later, Mrs. Bates once again awoke to the smell of smoke. The nightmare was repeating itself. This time they were cast ashore in Peru, but there the run of bad luck ended. The next ship carried the couple safely north to Panama, where they caught a ship bound for California.[9]

Crossing the Isthmus of Panama

Many Argonauts chose to sail by way of Panama instead of rounding Cape Horn. In those days before the Panama Canal was built, travelers crossed Panama by canoe and on mules. The choice made sense, because crossing the isthmus could cut travel time to a lightning quick four weeks. It was the land portion of the journey that took the greatest toll on the gold seekers. At Chagres, on Panama's Atlantic coast, the grandly named Crescent City Hotel turned out to be a bamboo hut. Both sexes shared a single large room. The women found the lack of privacy quite shocking, and morning did not improve matters. A noisy bunch

SOURCE DOCUMENT

PANAMA, NEW GRANADA, JAN. 7, 1849.

WHILE [AT CRUCES], CAPTAIN ELLIOTT, OF THE ARMY, A MR. BIRCH, OF NEW ORLEANS, A MR. LUCKETT, . . . AND THREE NATIVES DIED (IT IS SAID) OF ASIATIC CHOLERA, WHICH WAS RAGING WITH GREAT VIOLENCE AT NEW ORLEANS WHEN THE FALCON LEFT.

CAPTAIN ELLIOTT'S GRAVE WAS DUG WITH A FEW LITTLE STICKS AND AN EARTHEN BOWL, WHICH IS THE CUSTOM AT CRUCES. LUCKETT AND BIRTH DIED SOME TWO HOURS AFTER THEIR ATTACK; AND ONE OF THE NATIVES WHO WENT OUT TO SUGAR CANE, WENT TO HIS BED, AND DIED . . . IN THE MOST HORRIBLE CONVULSIONS, HAVING HAD, AS MR. BIRCH DID NOT, THE ORDINARY SYMPTOMS OF CHOLERA. . . .

FROM CRUCES TO PANAMA IS A DAY'S JOURNEY; AND IMMEDIATELY UPON YOUR ARRIVAL AT PANAMA YOU SHOULD CERTAINLY BATHE YOUR ENTIRE BODY IN BRANDY. . . . CHAGRES, LATOON, GORGONA, AND CRUCES ARE MUD PUDDLES, AND ABODES OF DEATH . . . WHERE FIVE SHAKES OF THE FEVER AND AGUE [MALARIA] SOMETIMES KILL. . . . EAT NO FRUIT WHATEVER; AVOID THE NIGHT AIR, &C; BUT WHEN YOU PASS THE GREAT HIGHWAY OF NATIONS FROM CRUCES TO PANAMA, YOU WILL ENCOUNTER DANGERS AND FATIGUES THAT WILL TRY THE STOUTEST HEART.[10]

Stephen Branch did his best to discourage travel to California by way of Panama. His dispatch, printed in the New York Herald, *painted a bleak picture of the dangers that awaited those who took the shortcut across the isthmus. Despite such warnings, thousands of Forty-Niners streamed across Panama during the Gold Rush. Cholera was the prime killer, but travelers also fell into ravines, drowned in the Chagres River, and died of yellow fever.*

of dogs, ducks, and pigs crowded into the dining room when the guests sat down to breakfast. Later, gliding up the Chagres River in a native canoe, Lucilla Brown regained her good humor. She was enchanted by the "flowers, birds of gay plumage flying hither and thither, the chattering of monkeys, the scream of parrots."[11]

As the novelty of jungle travel waned, the Argonauts complained about the heat, the heavy rains, and the high prices. They swatted at mosquitoes and worried about yellow fever. The overloaded canoes that ferried passengers up the sluggish river drew more protests. Argonauts sometimes forgot the discomfort of cramped seats when they saw alligators gliding through the muddy water. The river trip ended at a rough mountain trail that led to Panama City. The younger men walked the trail, but women were told to pull on pants and boots and ride astride their mules. In an age when women normally rode sidesaddle, this was a bold new experience. Younger children bounced along in hammocks slung between two mules.

The food served in Panama varied in its appeal. One Argonaut praised his breakfast of pork fat, fresh bread, and spring water. Fruit was plentiful, and the travelers dipped into their stockpile of ship's biscuits, coffee, and dried foods. For supper, another gold seeker made do with rice, fruit, and a "stew of bad meat." Hiram Pierce's hunting party bagged "Two wild turkeys, one monkey, one anteater, some pigeons, and one iguana." Monkey, the travelers learned, was a common dish in Panama. Jessie Frémont, wife of the explorer John C. Frémont, discovered that fact the hard way. At the village of Gorgona, the villagers proudly served her a breakfast of baked monkey. She managed to stay calm, even though the monkey "looked like a little child that had been burned to death."[12]

Fresh graves marked each mile of the isthmus route. The living rejoiced when they reached the Pacific, but their struggle was far from over. Ahead lay a long wait for a ship, and then another sea voyage. Their joy on reaching San Francisco must have been intense.

Landing in San Francisco

Newcomers to San Francisco were half convinced that the streets would be paved with gold. After all, was this not the entry port to the gold fields? The reality quickly reminded them that this was a frontier town. In summer dust rose in choking clouds as horse-drawn wagons rumbled along the unpaved streets. Winter rains left the wagons bogged down in seas of mud.

The rundown hotels and guest houses were not much better. Hotel clerks pointed guests toward rows of narrow bunks and told them to furnish their own bedding. The Argonauts slept in rooms with canvas walls and cloth ceilings. At night they sometimes awoke when rats scampered across their bedclothes. To save money, some Forty-Niners lived on ships abandoned in the harbor when their crews ran off to the gold fields. One woman kept a cow on board and made a nice profit selling cream and butter.

San Francisco's splendid harbor served as the main port of entry for gold seekers who arrived by sea. The Gold Rush was over when this photo was taken in 1900, but forests of bare masts were a familiar sight in 1849 and 1850. In those days, the harbor was filled with abandoned ships whose crews had run off to try their luck in the gold fields.

The price of food and lodging produced further shocks. Prices climbed day by day, sometimes hour by hour. A well-served dinner that cost a dollar in New York set diners back five dollars in San Francisco. A small loaf of bread sold for twenty-five cents, a week's room and board went for twenty-five dollars or more. Those who ran short of cash could borrow money—at an interest rate of 10 percent a month.[13]

As the newcomers settled in, a second side of the city emerged. Wherever the Forty-Niners looked, Californians were caught up in a frenzy of building, buying, and selling. If they were not playing poker or faro, they gambled on land, houses, foodstuffs, or mining tools. The talk was all about who had struck it rich, and where. A reporter studied the scene and concluded that San Francisco was full of madmen:

> A dozen times or more . . . I have been taken by the arm by some of the millionaires—so they call themselves, I call them madmen. . . . They have dragged me about, through the mud and filth almost up to my middle, from one pine box to another, called mansion, hotel, bank, or store, as it may please the imagination, and have told me . . . that these splendid . . . structures were theirs, and that they, the fortunate [owners] were worth from two to three hundred thousand dollars each.[14]

George Dornin remembered the first words he heard when his ship dropped anchor in the harbor. A man on Dornin's ship spied an old friend on the dock and called out, "Hallo, Bob! What's the news?"

The reply summed up the Gold Rush in just seven words. "Plenty of gold," Bob yelled back, "but hard to get!"[15]

★ SAILING UNDER A CLOUD OF CANVAS ★

The clipper ships were tall and beautiful—and they were fast. Builders designed their sleek hulls to glide smoothly through the water. The masts were set at rakish angles and masses of square-rigged canvas could be unfurled to catch the slightest breeze. Sharp-bowed and lean, the clippers sacrificed cargo space for speed. Navies used them to run down pirates and smugglers. Merchants chartered them to hurry their goods to distant markets.

The first true clipper ship was built in Baltimore in 1832. Built of spruce and oak, the *Ann McKim* was 143 feet long and weighed in at 493 tons. Blessed by good winds and calm seas, a clipper like the *McKim* could cover up to four hundred miles a day. The profits from a single speedy trip sometimes earned enough to pay the construction costs. With space at a premium, owners preferred to carry cargo instead of passengers.

The clippers won enduring fame during the Gold Rush. To make the 15,600-mile run from New York to San Francisco took most ships an average of six months. In 1850, the Sea Witch cut that time to ninety-seven days—and in 1851 the *Flying Cloud* set a record of eighty-nine days, twenty-one hours. A few months later, a second clipper made the return trip in seventy-six days. The proud captain asked to have the record carved on his tombstone.[16]

The men who sailed the clippers loved to brag about their ships. In time, some of their tall tales became part of the nation's folklore. One tale described the antics of Old Stormalong, who sailed on a clipper ship called the *Courser*. The ship was so big, Stormalong said, that sailors rode horseback across the decks while tending to their duties. The *Courser*'s captain was a tough old salt named

Tall and beautiful clipper ships set speed records on the world's oceans in the mid 1800s. In 1851, travelers marveled when the Flying Cloud *cut the six-month journey around Cape Horn to just three months.*

Ezekiel Macy Sims. To catch bluefish for his breakfast, Stormalong bragged, Captain Sims trained a swordfish to spear one for him each day.

The clipper ship soon passed into legend along with Old Stormalong. Freight rates fell during the late 1850s as steam engines began to take the place of sail. The final blow fell when a cross-isthmus railway opened in Panama. No longer profitable, the graceful clippers soon vanished from the shipping lanes.

5

LOOKING FOR THE ELEPHANT

The Forty-Niners told the story of a farmer who heard that the circus was coming to town. Happy at the thought of seeing his first elephant, he hitched up his wagon and set out. As he rolled into town a wonderful sight caught his eye. Shuffling along in front of the circus parade was a huge gray beast. Yes, it had to be an elephant! The sight thrilled the farmer, but spooked his horses. The team bolted, ran into a ditch, and overturned the wagon. Men came running to help, but the farmer waved them off. "I don't give a hang," he shouted, "for I have seen the elephant!"[1]

As they headed west on the California Trail, the emigrants dreamed of the wonders that lay ahead. "We're going to see the elephant," they shouted. Instead of fearing the dangers that lurked along the trail, they worried that they might miss a chapter in the great adventure. Margaret Frink remembered, "It appeared to me that none of the population had been left behind. . . . I thought, in my excitement, that if one-tenth of these teams and these people got ahead of us, there would be nothing left for us in California worth picking up."[2]

The numbers amazed the soldiers stationed at Fort Kearny. Their count showed that by July 1852, 25,855 men, 7,021 women, 8,270 children, and 2,166 wagons had passed the Nebraska fort. Legend says that most were scamps and rascals, the outcasts of polite society. Indeed, many looked the part. A St. Louis reporter wrote, "The ice is broken, and the gold diggers [are] upon us. The first specimen, with a large pick axe over his shoulder, a long rifle in his hand, and two revolvers and a bowie knife stuck in his belt, made his appearance here a week ago last Sunday. He only had time to ask for a drink of buttermilk, a piece of gingerbread, and how 'fur' it was to 'Californy.'"[3]

Despite these tales, solid citizens outnumbered the gamblers, crooks, wastrels, and drunks eight to one. If these upright gold seekers had a fault, it was their misreading of the perils that lay ahead. All they knew for certain was that the overland route was shorter and cheaper than sea travel. Many already owned the household goods, wagons, and livestock needed for the journey.

Emigrants who lacked the pioneer spirit soon turned back. Others fell ill, or injured themselves. A few gambled away the money they needed to buy supplies. Sarah Royce, who traveled west with her husband in 1849, saw the problem clearly. "It soon became plain," she wrote in her diary, "that the hard facts of this pilgrimage would require patience, energy, and courage." Looking deep inside herself as the long,

Each mile along the trail offered new challenges to both travelers and livestock. In this 1883 photo, weary drovers and their equally weary ox teams plod westward through a desolate stretch of western terrain.

hard days passed, she took a quiet joy in her own strength. Her diary records the "mildly exultant feeling which comes from having kept silent through a cowardly fit, and finding the fit gone off."[4]

Following the California Trail

Once they said good-bye to friends who were continuing along the Oregon Trail, emigrants needed all the strength they could muster. Ahead lay the California Trail and the maze of trails and cutoffs blazed by trappers, traders, and mountain men (see map, page 35). The leaders of each wagon train had to make their own best guess as to what route to take. In the early days, most followed the Truckee route that Elisha Stephens had opened in the spring of 1844.

Before the Stephens party of twenty-three men, eight women, and fifteen children made the journey, no one had taken wagons over the Sierra Nevada mountains. After leaving South Pass, Stephens led his caravan west across the Sublette Cutoff to Fort Hall. From there he followed the Humboldt River to the point where it vanished in the desert sand. Fortune smiled on Stephens at that point, for he met a friendly American Indian named Truckee. It was Truckee who showed him a safe way to cross the Forty-Mile Desert. The next leg followed a river (later named the Truckee River in the guide's honor) to the site of present-day Reno, Nevada. From there the party made it over Donner Pass after hauling five of the wagons up a thousand-foot granite slope. By the spring of 1845, Stephens and his party were relaxing in the warmth of the Sacramento Valley. The California Trail was open for business.

In 1849, some 22,500 gold seekers set out for California along the Oregon-California Trail. Fast-growing towns—such as Independence and St. Joseph, Missouri, as well as Council Bluffs, Iowa—served as jumping-off points. Ahead lay nearly two thousand miles of prairie, desert, and mountains. There were rivers to cross, cliffs to climb, and breakdowns to repair. Travelers who harbored doubts or fears were advised to keep them quiet.

The first leg across the prairie followed the Platte and Sweetwater Rivers. Ten days after crossing the North Fork, the emigrants caught sight of massive Independence Rock. After stopping to carve their names in the soft stone, they moved on to South Pass. There the Forty-Niners said good-bye to friends bound for Oregon and turned south to skirt the Great Salt Lake. A zigzag route across Utah and Nevada led to the Humboldt River and the desolate Humboldt Sink. The sink was a marshy basin at the western end of the Humboldt River where the salty water eventually sank into the sandy soil. Everyone filled their water kegs before setting out across the Forty-Mile Desert.

Days and nights spent slogging through sand took the wagons trains to the cool waters of the Carson River. One traveler wrote that he camped that night under a cottonwood—the first tree he had seen in seven hundred miles.[5] Now only the Sierra Nevada Mountains lay between the emigrants and their goal. An exhausting climb to Carson Pass completed the first stage of that final leg. Four days later, if all went well, the wagon trains rolled into the Sacramento Valley.

The Forty-Niners put their faith in guidebooks that were far from trustworthy. Sarah Royce and her husband carried a two-page, hand-written guide when they left Salt Lake City. On the first page, Ira Willis assured his readers that this was the "Best Guide to the Gold Mines: 816 Miles." After describing the route to the Humboldt Sink, Willis dropped in a comment typical of the guidebooks of the day. There might be a new track across the mountains, he wrote, "that Childs [a mountain man] intended to make last fall."[6]

A second well-known guidebook was equally vague. In *The Emigrants' Guide to Oregon and California*, Lansford Hastings described the Sierras as a minor barrier. "Wagons can be as readily taken from Ft. Hall to the bay of St. Francisco, as they can, from the States to Ft. Hall," the guide promised. "In fact, the latter part of the route is found much [easier] for a wagon than the former."[7] To those who trusted Hastings, the dangerous mountain passage must have come as a terrible shock.

Making Ready for the Long Trek

Each wagon train wrote its own story of the great trek west. Some, blessed by good weather and good health, enjoyed fairly easy trips. William Kelly's company left Independence on April 16, 1849, and reached the gold fields on July 26. No one dared start much earlier. Spring rains could turn placid streams into raging torrents. Starting too early also meant that the mules and oxen would find the prairie grasses too sparse for good grazing.

Only a few caravans came close to matching Kelly's record time for the journey. Sarah Royce's family started from Iowa on April 30—and did not reach the Sacramento Valley until October 21. Among other dangers, their slow progress exposed them to severe mountain weather. Royce's diary entry for October 18

Fort Bridger was a welcome sight to caravans worn out by weeks of travel across the plains. A stop at the remote Wyoming trading post gave settlers a chance to repair their wagons, buy supplies, and ask about conditions on the trail ahead.

reads: "That night we slept within a few yards of snow, which lay in a ravine. Water froze in our pans not very far from the fire." To her great joy, the next morning dawned bright and sunny. The long trek was nearly over. A few hours later Sarah looked down on what she called the "smiling face" of California.[8]

The Forty-Niners carried as much food as they could manage. One group of five men stocked their wagons with one thousand pounds of sea biscuits, two hundred pounds of flour, one hundred pounds of cornmeal, six hundred pounds of bacon, one hundred pounds of coffee, one hundred pounds of sugar, and twenty pounds of tea.[9] The emigrants also packed vinegar, pickles, smoked beef, and cheese. Those who could afford them added sardines and other canned goods. In some regions nature helped set the table. Men hunted buffalo, deer, bears, and waterfowl, and fished for trout and catfish. Women and children gathered berries, wild onions, green peas, and a tender leaf known as lamb's lettuce.

For the most part, the gold seekers dressed as they had at home. Each item of clothing should be warm and durable, one guidebook advised. At night everyone rolled up in blankets. Children slept in the wagons, the adults in tents or in the open. For hunting and for protection, the men carried rifles, pistols, and knives. Some preferred flintlock rifles, but many shelled out twenty-five dollars or more for a fast-loading percussion-cap rifle. Other useful articles that found their way into the wagons included axes, hammers, nails, needles, soap, thread, wax, rope, and candles.[10]

The Conestoga wagons used on the Santa Fe Trail were too heavy for the California Trail. The Forty-Niners drove light farm wagons that carried a ton or more of food, clothing, tools, tents, and other gear. One man wrote home to say he paid fifty-eight dollars for a "pretty good" used wagon. About ten feet long, these small wagons were easier to handle, even when fully loaded. If the wagon box was watertight, it could be floated across a river. Some men built a raised floor above the bed of the wagon to provide extra storage space. Bowed hickory rods held up a five-foot-high canvas top that sheltered riders from sun, wind, and rain. Unlike pack mules, these "homes on wheels" did not have to be unloaded each night. They also served as ambulances for the sick and injured.

With the wagons loaded, it was time to go. Drivers hitched up teams of mules (up to seventy-five dollars a head) or oxen (around fifty dollars a pair) and hit the trail.

Life on the Trail

Safety on the long trek to California lay in numbers. Most of the Forty-Niners traveled with a caravan of ten to twelve wagons. Large parties of forty wagons or more often split up after a few weeks. Smaller groups, the gold seekers soon realized, moved faster and got by with less bickering. Each company elected a captain who picked the route and settled disputes. The travelers also agreed to rules that governed their lives on the trail. One common rule called for the emigrants to keep Sunday as a day of rest and worship. Like the strict discipline that some captains tried to enforce, the Sunday rule often was ignored. Taking Sundays off became a luxury as worries mounted that the caravan might not reach California before snow closed the mountain passes.

A wagon train covered about fourteen miles on an average day. With a river to cross or breakdowns to repair, progress could slow to a mile or two. The

While traveling along the trail in Wyoming, Forty-Niners celebrated when the massive dome of Independence Rock came into view. After setting up camp nearby, settlers often carved their names into the great rock. Some of the names are still visible, including Elias and Mary Morris, who reached the landmark on September 12, 1852.

danger of overloaded wagons became clear as soon as the trail turned muddy. As the wheels sank into muck, drivers cracked their whips and screamed at the oxen to pull harder. Other men cursed and put their shoulders to the iron-tired wheels. Before long, the lesson learned, families lightened their wagons. One company threw out "a considerable amount of clothing, a fair-sized library, two bushels of beans, two pigs of lead [for making bullets], half a keg of nails, a plow, and a lot of mechanical tools."[11]

At daybreak the men and boys rounded up any of the livestock that had strayed. When the order came to move out, the wagon drivers found their places in line. After a day in the lead, drivers moved to the rear and worked their way forward again. That arrangement was judged fair, because in dry weather the last wagons in line rolled through dust clouds kicked up by the lead wagons. At midmorning the captain gave the order to stop for breakfast. If the women had wood or buffalo chips for a fire, they baked biscuits, fried bacon, and brewed coffee. The men fed the stock and laid in grass and water. By two o'clock the wagons were rolling again.

As night fell the drivers pulled the wagons into a half circle that formed a pen for the livestock. Families pitched their tents beside their wagons, well clear of a possible stampede. Guards took up stations on the open side to keep the animals from straying. The dogs that trotted beside the wagons all day joined them at their posts. Some were well trained, but many "were worthless curs, . . . pestering the cattle and horses by day, and keeping people awake at night with senseless barking and howling."[12]

After supper, the Forty-Niners gathered near the campfires to sing, dance, and tell stories. For Lydia Waters, one of these quiet nights turned into a nightmare. Her wagon train was camped on the Wood River in Nebraska when a thunderstorm struck. After the storm passed, she learned that "a Mr. Myers . . . was found sitting on the front seat [of a wagon] dead. . . . I kept a lock of his hair which was burnt off by the lightning and gave it to his wife some days afterward."[13]

Young Peter Decker summed up the challenge all Forty-Niners faced: "There is surely no Royal road to California & traveling it is labor indeed," he wrote.[14]

SOURCE DOCUMENT

SATURDAY, AUGUST 11 [1849]

Twelve miles upon the old road brought us to the Sink, . . . [which] extends over several miles & is generally grown up with rushes & grass. . . . The road keeps in [the Sink's] basins, which extend over *miles & miles* without a vestige of vegetation, but so white & dazzling in the sun as scarcely to be looked at. We rolled by this, the water of which cannot be used by man or beast, [for] 4 miles, & came to some sulphur springs or rather wells. Here we encamped for the night. The animals drank [from the sulphur springs] freely & it seemed to do them no harm. . . . The most obnoxious, hideous gases perfumed our camp all night, arising from the many dead animals around. Distance: 23 miles.

SUNDAY, AUGUST 12

We rolled out at daybreak. . . . In four miles we came to the forks of the road. Here we found many placards [signs], the most of which advised their friends to take the right. The left was but little traveled in comparison to the right, & we took it. . . . [A]t 10 miles we stopped to breakfast, which was cooked with some pieces of wagon we picked up on the road. We layed by until 2 o'clock having given grass & water to our stock, & again rolled. . . . We rolled thus 15 miles, which brought us to the Hot Springs. . . .

These hot springs are one of The things upon this earth. . . . A piece of meat, held in one [of] the boiling springs, boiled in 20 minutes, perfectly done. By putting the water in your coffee-pot & holding the pot over the bubbling, it would boil in a few minutes. In this way many of us cooked our suppers.

Thousands of dollars worth of property thrown away by the emigration was laying here. . . . The machinery of a turning machine that must have cost $600 or $700. A steam engine & machinery for coining that could not have cost less than $2000 or $3000, were also laying here, all sacrificed upon this Jornada. These things they say belonged to the notorious Mr. Finley (?) who also lost 55 cattle out of 80. Distance: 25 miles.[15]

Wakeman Bryarly made these entries in his diary while traveling the California Trail in 1849. His first sight of the desolate region around the Humboldt Sink filled him with awe, but did not daunt him. He knew a greater challenge lay ahead—the scorching Forty-Mile Desert and the towering peaks of the Sierra Nevada.

★ THE GREAT DEBATE: MULES VS. OXEN ★

The Forty-Niners did not doubt the wisdom of using wagons to carry their equipment and supplies. The real debate began when they picked animals to pull their wagons. Should they buy horses, mules, or oxen?

Experts agreed that horses were faster than oxen and stronger than mules. When asked to pull heavy loads over rough trails, however, horses sometimes broke down. Horses also needed a daily ration of grain to keep up their strength. Making room in the wagons for feed sacks meant less room for people and supplies.

The great debate, therefore, matched mules against oxen. Take a seat at the campfire and listen to how Mike and Ollie might go at it.

Mike: Mules get you where you're going faster.

Ollie: Yeah, but a good team of oxen can pull more weight. And oxen don't stampede so easy.

Mike: That may be. But when they do get loose, your dad-blamed oxen will run till they drop. Those critters don't know when to stop.

Ollie: Mules bog down a heap worse in the mud.

Mike: Sure, but what if the grass runs out? Mules can live on cottonwood bark.

Ollie: Well, just wait 'til you run into a band of Sioux warriors. They'll steal mules in a wink, but they don't have much use for oxen.

Mike [tapping his rifle]: Don't worry about the Sioux. Just remember that oxen will be stumbling along on sore feet when mules are still going strong.[16]

In this 1871 photo, newspaper reporter Fred Loring posed next to Evil Merodach, his favorite mule. Loring died soon afterward, cut down by Apache raiders while traveling across Arizona.

For many gold seekers, the choice came down to the cost. A good mule could set them back seventy-five dollars, the price of three oxen. Because money was tight, most Forty-Niners settled for the placid, slow-moving oxen.

Out on the trail, both animals performed well when they were properly handled. As one Forty-Niner wrote of his mules, "It was a noble sight to see those small, tough, honest Spanish mules, every nerve strained to the utmost, examples of obedience, and of duty performed under trying circumstances." Another man blessed his ox teams for being patient, durable, gentle, and easily driven. "Those who come to this country will be in love with their oxen by the time they reach here," he concluded.[17]

6

"THE ROAD WAS LINED WITH SKELETONS"

The Forty-Niners headed west "to see the elephant" with high hopes. If they had worries, they mostly centered on fears of being attacked by American Indians. Few doubted their ability to cross the nearly trackless wilderness. Jessy Thornton noted that the men "cracked their whips and cracked their jokes." Everyone seemed "cheerful and happy," he wrote, and many were "almost boisterous in their mirth."[1]

Young Susan Thompson agreed that life on the trail was delightful. "We were a happy, carefree, lot of young people and the dangers and hardships found no resting place on our shoulders," she wrote. "It was a continuous picnic and excitement was plentiful." During noontime halts, "we ran races or made swings. There was plenty of frolic."[2] At night the emigrants gathered around their campfires after chores were done. Someone would pick out a tune on a banjo. Everyone joined in on the chorus of "Ho! For California:"

We've formed our band and we're all well-manned
To journey afar to the promised land,
Where the golden ore is rich in store,
On the banks of the Sacramento shore.
   Then, ho! Boys ho! To California go.
   There's plenty of gold in the world we're told
   On the banks of the Sacramento.[3]

Gradually, the singing died away. The trail was rough, and there were rivers and ravines to cross. American Indian horsemen appeared out of nowhere to brandish weapons and demand gifts. Thunderstorms toppled tents and stampeded livestock. Illness and accidents took their toll. A newspaper reporter's tongue-in-cheek advice began to take on a new meaning:

> If you are determined to come [to California], . . . try an experiment as follows: take a blanket and go to the top of the highest hill when the wind blows fresh. Take a stone for your pillow, and pebbles for feathers; sleep here a few nights. Then go, when it rains, where the ground is wet, and the weather cold. When you get used to this, try flour and water and jerked beef for food, once a day; then go without either until you get so hungry that you can eat moldy bread and say that it is good. When you get used to this, work in the water up to your middle, and say gold will compensate you for it. If you can endure all this, I advise you to come—but not till then.[4]

The warning was lost in the sound of wagons rolling westward. The stream of emigrants never faltered, despite the alarming stories that filtered back from the frontier.

Rigors of the Plains

The Forty-Niners soon lost count of the hazards that came their way. A few could be brushed aside. If firewood ran short, the women gathered buffalo chips. When mosquitoes swarmed to the attack, men built smoky fires to chase them away. Other obstacles, such as the rivers and mountains that lay in their path, could be conquered through hard work and invention. Finally, there were hardships that must be endured, like rain, heat, dust, and wind. A sudden storm could drop six inches of rain and leave wagons stuck deep in mud.

The fierce windstorms that swept across the plains sometimes ripped the canvas from wagons and panicked livestock. In this engraving, a Kansas farmer tries to quiet his horses while his wife clings to her seat in the wagon. Even though westbound settlers used heavier rigs, storms of this strength wrecked many wagons.

A week later each drop of water would be precious, as the wagons rolled across a sun-baked plain.

Once the travelers were under way, troubles seemed to come in bunches. Because springs and brakes were almost unknown, the wagons rattled and jolted over the rough ground. The most common breakdowns came when a wheel hit a rock or a driver lost control on a downhill grade. Sudden shocks snapped wagon tongues and shattered axles. (The tongue is the harnessing pole that is attached to the

SOURCE DOCUMENT

DIARY ENTRIES BY DELOS ASHLEY, 1849

TUES. JULY 17 VERY WARM—SAND ROADS. TOILSOME AS HELL.

WEDNES J 18 SAND!!! HOT!!! GRASS PARCHED & DRY—

P.M. 10 MS OF R[IVER] CAMP 8 P.M.

THURS JULY 19 CAMPED 10 P.M. NO GRASS (WHEUGH!!!!)

FRI. JULY 20, 10 O'C HOT!!! NO HALT AT NOON.

CAMPED 6 O'C P.M. GRASS 3 MS. SPRING AT SLOUGH.

SAT. JULY 21 STAID AT SLOUGH

SUN. JULY 22 FROM SLEW TO SINK (O BARRENNESS)[5]

Forty-niner Delos Ashley dreaded the heat that baked his wagon train as it crawled along the Humboldt River. That leg of the journey was a picnic, however, compared to the Forty-Mile Desert that lay beyond the Humboldt Sink. In a later entry, Ashley jotted down (but did not explain) this brief entry: "Slept in the Sun & was near killed."

front axle of a wagon drawn by horses, mules, or oxen.) If the wagon carried spare parts, repairs could be made quickly. More often, the men had to hack a new tongue or axle out of a handy tree.

Good wagons were useless without healthy live-stock to pull them. The Forty-Niners, despite their best efforts, littered the trail with dead horses, cattle, mules, and oxen. Weaker animals broke down under the stress of pulling overloaded wagons. Emigrants who started late could expect to see grasslands cropped bare by the herds that had gone before. On the high plains and in the desert, animals weakened by hunger and thirst often collapsed and died.

Disaster sometimes struck at night, just when the camp seemed most secure. A sudden crash of thunder or the scent of buffalo could stampede a herd. The frightened animals would crash through the wall of wagons and rush blindly into the darkness. At day-break, weary men rode out to gather the scattered stock. All too often they brought back bad news. Wolves might have pulled down an ox or two. Horses broke their legs when they stepped into prairie dog holes. If American Indians were camped nearby, they might well have butchered a couple of wandering cows.

Thirsty travelers welcomed the sight of rivers and streams. Fording them was another matter. To prepare for a crossing, the men nailed boards across the wagon boxes. Women and children climbed onto the raised platforms and the men took up their stations with the oxen. The drivers did their best to steady the animals and keep them moving through the muddy water. Men mounted on horses held ropes tied high on the upstream side of each wagon. Tugging on the ropes kept the current from overturning the wagon and its precious cargo. Hundreds of wagons crossed the South Fork of the Platte in this way. Emigrants joked that fording the broad river was like embarking on a sea voyage.

Near present-day Casper, Wyoming, a ferry hauled wagons across the broad, deep waters of the North Platte. The Mormon ferrymen charged seventy-five cents to four dollars per wagon. For additional fees they also shoed mules and repaired wagons. The "ferry" was little more than a large raft, but it carried hundreds of wagons across the river. One Forty-Niner moaned as he paid the price: "The Mormons . . . have as good a gold mine here as any in California."[6]

Crossing Deserts and Mountains

Most Forty-Niners looked on river crossings as child's play compared to crossing the desert. Wagon trains hit the Forty-Mile Desert at a time when spirits were sagging and animals were worn out. The ordeal began at the Humboldt Sink, where the emigrants halted to cut grass and fill their water barrels. The wise old hands knew that it was best to take the crossing in one long haul. The emigrants started early one morning and plodded forward through the heat and sand. The leaders called halts only to rest the oxen and mules. Mirages taunted the travelers with images of cool lakes and green meadows.

Because of low water levels, the North Fork of the Platte River was easily forded late in the summer. But in the spring, when most caravans reached this point, the river was in full flow. A group of enterprising Mormons helped keep the wagons moving by running a ferry service on the Platte.

A long day and half a night of desert travel brought the wagon trains to the Boiling Springs. The springs were both welcome and dreadful, for they stank of sulphur and sent bubbling geysers into the air. Damming the flow created pools of cooler water that thirsty oxen could drink. After a brief rest, the emigrants trudged up a sand-covered ridge. Weary oxen sank knee-deep into the soft sand, and wagon wheels shuddered to a stop. As anxious drivers prodded and screamed, a few of the weaker oxen dropped to their knees and died. From the top of the ridge the going was easier. Everyone breathed a sigh of relief when a grove of cottonwoods appeared in the distance. A final sagebrush-covered slope led down to the Truckee River. Lydia Waters wrote of that moment, "If I ever saw Heaven, I saw it then."[7]

Luzena Wilson was one of the travelers who made that forced march across the desert. The burning images found their way into her journal:

> The hot earth scorched our feet; the grayish dust hung about us like a cloud, making our eyes red, and tongues parched, and our thousand bruises and scratches smart like burns. The road was lined with the skeletons of the poor beasts who had died in the struggle. . . . Sometimes we found the bones of men bleaching beside their broken-down and abandoned wagons. The buzzards and coyotes, driven away by our presence from their horrible feasting, hovered just out of reach.[8]

With the desert behind them, the Forty-Niners rested and repaired their gear. Ahead lay a final hurdle, the high passes of the Sierra Nevada mountains. The men tackled the steepest climbs by hitching as many as a dozen yoke of oxen to a single wagon. Once the panting beasts reached the top, the men led the teams back to pull up yet another wagon. After dragging all the wagons to the top, they fastened chains to the back of the first wagon and began the perilous descent. Wrapping the chains around trees and rocks helped the men keep control on the steep grade. Link by link, they eased each wagon down to level ground. That

SOURCE DOCUMENT

EPITAPHS FOUND ON GRAVESITES
ALONG THE CALIFORNIA TRAIL

M. DE MORST,
OF COL[UMBUS]: OHIO,
DIED SEP. 16TH, 1849
AGED 50 YEARS,
OF CAMP FEVER

JNO. A. DAWSON,
ST. LOUIS, MO.
DIED OCT. 1ST, 1849
FROM EATING A POISONOUS
ROOT AT THE SPRING.

IN MEMORY OF SAMUEL OLIVER
OF WAUKESHA, WISCONSIN,
WHO WAS KILLED BY AN ARROW SHOT
FROM A PARTY OF INDIANS, JULY 5TH, 1850
WHILE STANDING GUARD AT NIGHT.

JNO. HOOVER, DIED, JUNE 18, '49
AGED 12 YRS. REST IN PEACE,
SWEET BOY, FOR THY TRAVELS ARE OVER.

The graves that lined the California Trail bore witness to Forty-Niners who lost their battle with the wilderness. As these epitaphs remind us, death came in many forms. The dreaded cholera, in particular, swept away entire family groups. One sad epitaph said all there was to say about the dangers of the trail: Died: Mrs. Emmaline Barnes, Amanda and Mahela Robbins, three sisters in one grave, Indiana.[9]

technique was useless when sheer cliffs barred the way. The emigrants conquered the cliffs by unloading the wagons and taking them apart. Then they used a windlass to raise or lower trunks, barrels, and wagon parts to the next level.

As they climbed higher, the Forty-Niners shivered in mountain cold. William Swain awoke one morning to find that snow had fallen during the night. When he tried to rouse the oxen, sixteen of them lay dead. He guessed that they suffocated after ice clogged their nostrils. On another morning he wrote, "It is a bad day . . . snowing, cold, and cheerless. We started late this morning."[10] Swain should have counted his blessings. In 1846, an early snowfall trapped the Donner party in those same mountains. By the time rescue arrived in the spring, forty people had perished.

A Trail Lined with Graves

Rough terrain, bad weather, and American Indian arrows took their toll on the Forty-Niners. Disease, however, was the reason for most of the graves that lined the trail. Weakened by hard work and a poor diet, the emigrants fell victim to fevers, cholera, scurvy, and other ills. To make matters worse, companies could not afford lengthy stops to nurse the sick and injured. William Swain complained, "It is indeed hard to be sick in a wagon while traveling under the burning sun." His friends, he wrote, are "so blunted by weariness that they will not take the trouble to administer to your comfort."[11]

Once again, the deadliest killer was cholera. Spread through unclean food and water, the disease raced through whole wagon trains. Youth and good health were no defense. Victims fell ill with severe diarrhea, vomiting, muscle cramps, and cold sweats. Doctors did what they could, but medical practice in those days was more guesswork than science. A typical treatment consisted of doses of laudanum (a form of opium) and rubdowns with brandy. For many emigrants, a bout with cholera was a death sentence.

Sarah Royce stood by helplessly as cholera sent a fellow traveler into convulsions. After the old man died, she spent a sleepless night watching over her daughter Mary. The next day, hoping to stop the spread of the disease, the Royces scrubbed the wagon and all its contents. The effort seemed wasted when news came that two more men had fallen ill. "Who

The trail across arid wasteland such as the Forty-Mile Desert was marked by the skeletons of dead livestock. A few of the animals fell victim to American Indian arrows, but most died of hunger, thirst, and exhaustion.

would go next?" Sarah wondered. "What if my husband should be taken and leave us alone in the wilderness?" In that dark moment Sarah wrote in her diary, "I poured out my heart to God in prayer, and He gave me comfort and rest." Before long word came that one of the men had died, but the other was feeling better. Sarah relaxed a little. "From that time we had no more cases of cholera among our fellow travelers," she wrote.[12]

Cholera was a major worry, but it was not the only danger on the trail. Lydia Waters wrote in her diary about the day her wagon cover caught fire. While a friend ran for water, Lydia grabbed handfuls of damp tea leaves from the teapot and "patted on the fire. The wind was very strong, but I almost had it out when the water came. . . . My hands were so scorched that they did not get well for two months."[13] Lydia was lucky that her burns did not become infected. A nine-year-old boy developed gangrene after a wagon wheel crushed his leg. A former surgeon's helper offered to try to save the boy's life by amputating the leg. After a dose of laudanum, the amateur surgeon set to work with a butcher knife and a handsaw. The operation took almost two hours—by which time the boy had died of shock and loss of blood.[14]

Livestock suffered alongside their masters. Oxen fell sick more often than did mules, who seemed to know better than to drink bad water. One time-tested treatment sometimes saved oxen that collapsed after drinking alkali-tainted spring water. William Swain writes that "we then tied pieces of fat bacon to the ends of sticks . . . and shoved it down the throats of the suffering creatures. It formed a sort of soap in their stomachs which neutralized the effect of the alkali."[15]

Weary and footsore, the Forty-Niners pushed on. When food stocks ran low, they ate "rancid bacon with the grease fried out by the hot sun, musty flour, and bits of bread well coated with alkali."[16] Hunters stalked deer and bison, but sometimes settled for hawks and jackrabbits. One teenager watched her mother fall sick after drinking a bowl of coyote soup. Another wagon train found a woman who had been stranded by the death of her husband. She and her children survived, she told her rescuers, by eating the bark of a tree.[17]

★ THE DONNER PARTY: "NEVER TAKE NO CUTOFS" ★

The year was 1846. At a time when most emigrants were heading for Oregon, one wagon train aimed for California. Most of the men who rode beside the wagons that carried their wives and children were well-to-do farmers and merchants. As captain, the families picked a farmer named George Donner.

Just beyond South Pass, the Donner party left the Oregon Trail. From Fort Bridger they took a new cutoff that Lansford Hastings had described in a popular guidebook. By this time the party numbered some eighty-seven men, women, and children. None of them knew that no one had ever taken wagons over the Hastings cutoff.

From that day on the party's problems multiplied. The Wasatch Range was heavily wooded, and the men of the Donner party had to hack out a trail for the wagons. In fifteen days they traveled only thirty-six miles. That ordeal led to a desert crossing that proved to be forty miles longer than Hastings had promised. Even the Humboldt River gave little relief. Cattle wandered off in the night and were stolen by Paiute warriors. The need to keep moving bred a kind of panic. When one old man could no longer walk, the party left him behind to die.

Wintry weather added to the difficulty of driving wagons across the Sierra Nevada Mountains. In this drawing, rescuers dig out a family whose mountain cabin was buried by deep snow. Caught in a similar trap, the Donner party resorted to cannibalism to survive.

At Truckee Meadows, the group rested for five days. By the time they started up to what is now called Donner Pass, snow was falling. A long, hard climb took them to the pass, but at that point they bogged down in deep snow. Unable to advance or retreat, they took shelter in tents and crude huts near Donner Lake. Day by day, the snow drifted deeper and deeper. Six small groups volunteered to go for help. Only one half-frozen band made it through to the Sacramento Valley.

Animals died, and their bodies disappeared beneath the snow. Women boiled hides and gave the soggy chunks to children to chew on. The death toll began to mount. What happened next still horrifies readers a century and a half later. Patrick Breen, one of the survivors, told the story:

> Feb. 26, Hungry times in camp, plenty of hides but the folks will not eat them, . . . Mrs. Murphy said here yesterday that she thought she would commence on Milton and eat him. I do not think she has done so yet, it is so distressing. The Donners told the California folks four days ago that they would commence on the dead people if they did not succeed that day or next in finding their cattle, then ten or twelve feet under the snow.[18]

A relief party reached the survivors just five days later. Of the eighty-seven people who began the trek, only forty-seven survived. One of them, twelve-year-old Virginia Reed, sent some wise advice to her cousin soon after her rescue. "[N]ever," she wrote, "take no cutofs and hury along as fast as you can."[19]

7

THE TRAIL PROSPERS... AND DIES

Every wagon train that rolled into the Sacramento Valley had stories to tell. A few of the gold seekers could boast of making a safe and speedy journey. More often, the emigrants limped the last few miles, worn down by their months in the wilderness.

William Swain took a moment to study his companions after twenty-five weeks on the trail. The men who stared back at him were "footsore, lantern-jawed skeletons." His diary entry went on, "Our journey is done, and we hardly know what to do with ourselves. . . . There will be no more Indian alarms; no more stampedes; no more pulling, carrying, and hauling at wagons. . . . We are in rags, almost barefooted, without provisions. . . . But however sad for the fate of the poor fellows who fell by the way, we are glad to have got here at all."[1]

The strenuous journey turned out to be good training for the gold fields. The Forty-Niners had been toughened by their ordeal. Their hands were callused and their arms were strong. They were used to sleeping in the open. For breakfast they could make do with

★ 87 ★

hard biscuits fried in bacon fat. By contrast, the idle months at sea did little to prepare the Argonauts for what lay ahead. To find gold meant digging and more digging. Their spirits were willing, but a few days of digging blistered their hands and strained their backs.

Change Comes to the Trail

Most men raced for the gold fields as soon as their wagons rumbled over the last mountain ridges. Peter Burnett, who later served as California's first governor, took his time. Late in 1848, after asking around for advice, he bought a claim on the Yuba River. The Yuba, however, did not give up its gold easily. Burnett and his two partners rose at dawn, ate breakfast, and worked until noon. After a half-hour break for lunch they went back to their claim and toiled until sundown. At night they slept on the hard ground under a canvas tent. "Within about three or four days we were [each] making twenty dollars daily," Burnett later wrote, "and we soon paid for our claim."[2]

Like most gold seekers, Burnett never struck it rich. After six weeks of prospecting he left the river and started a law practice at Sutter's Fort. His vantage point at the end of the trail gave him a chance to watch California grow. In 1850, nearly forty-five thousand emigrants took to the California Trail. The numbers fell in 1851, but rebounded in 1852. In that busy year, over fifty thousand men, women, and children headed west to build new lives on the far side of the mountains.[3]

Old-timers grumbled that the trail was turning into a "gol-durned turnpike."

Heavy traffic smoothed out some of the roughest spots on the trail. Sharp turns gave way to gentle curves, making the trail seem more like a road. New ferries and bridges made river crossings easier. Trading posts opened to sell flour, bacon, and other supplies. As another sign of changing times, the army set up a post office at South Pass. Emigrants gladly paid the dollar postage to mail letters home from that remote spot. In 1857, Congress budgeted $300,000 (a huge sum in those days) to pay for further improvements.

Change came quickly to the western territories. By the 1860s, express lines were running Concord stagecoaches over routes once dominated by covered wagons. As this 1869 photo demonstrates, soldiers were called on to ride shotgun atop the stagecoaches.

Surveyors laid out gentler grades, and work crews spanned rivers with sturdy bridges. In Nevada, engineers built new reservoirs to provide water for the desert crossing.

By 1850, most of the wagon trains were following the Carson route. Canny wagon bosses stayed clear of the treacherous Lassen route, which they called Lassen's Horn Route. Like Cape Horn, the nickname implied, that was the long way around. Caravans headed for Carson Pass could look forward to ending their desert trek at a new trading post called Ragtown. The scattered piles of worn-out clothing the emigrants discarded there had inspired the name. Further along the trail lay Mormon Station, a second resupply point. Travelers groused about high prices, but no one with ready money passed up the chance to buy supplies.

As the trail improved, the makeup of the wagon trains changed as well. In 1849, ox teams pulled about 80 percent of the wagons. Within the year, the balance started to shift. Later emigrants hitched horses to 55 percent of the wagons, mules to 25 percent, and oxen to only 20 percent. Horse-drawn wagons covered ground faster, but the big horses needed grain to keep up their strength. To make room for feed sacks, drivers hitched their teams to bigger wagons. Blessed with an improved trail and more horsepower, the gold seekers made better time. As early as 1850, a wagon train drawn by mule teams reached the end of the trail in only seventy-six days.[4]

Encounters with American Indians

The trail was changing, but one constant remained. The settlers did not get along with American Indians—nor, for the most part, did they try. Raised on gory tales of massacres and scalpings, the Forty-Niners viewed the "redskins" with alarm. In truth, American Indians had better reason to fear the newcomers. Records show that 250,000 emigrants crossed the plains between 1840 and 1860—and only 362 died at the hands of the land's first settlers. During that same twenty-year span, westbound emigrants killed 426 American Indians.[5] Cholera, the trail's most active killer, ignored skin color. The disease felled at least fifteen hundred emigrants and a far greater number of American Indians.

Much of the route to South Pass led through Indian Territory. This was land the government had set aside for the western tribes. The Shawnee and other peaceful tribes often supplied the emigrants with horses and wild game. Farther west, the once-fierce Pawnee could have been a threat. Tribal wars and disease, however, had greatly weakened them. In 1849 alone, cholera spread by the wagon trains wiped out over twelve hundred Pawnee. As one Forty-Niner wrote, "We are armed to the teeth, but . . . because of cholera, we could hardly get a sight of [the Pawnee]. . . . Our arms are useless, for we carry with us in their imagination a protection more formidable: the dread scourge which has spread among them."[6]

The settlers sometimes made use of the American Indian's fear of the white man's diseases. One story tells of a wagon train whose outriders saw a lone scout approaching. The riders rode back to the wagons to warn that the scout would likely be followed by a war party. Hoping to avoid a shootout, a quick-thinking doctor dusted a freckle-faced boy with flour. When he was finished, the boy's freckles showed dark against his floured skin. Later, as the scout approached, the doctor pointed to his "patient" and shouted, "Smallpox! Smallpox!" The warning, confirmed by the sight of the "spots" on the boy's face, did the job. The scout wheeled his horse and raced off to tell his companions to keep their distance.[7]

In Hollywood films American Indians attack every wagon train that comes their way. In real life, attacks by circling bands of warriors were rare. Instead of providing easy targets for the settlers' rifles, the tribes carried on a guerrilla war. William Swain complained that along the Humboldt River hardly a night passed without a Paiute raid on the livestock. "If they cannot drive the animals off," he wrote, "they creep up behind the sage bushes in the night and shoot arrows into them, so that the animals have to be left."[8] More often, American Indians crowded into emigrant camps and begged or demanded food. Most travelers agreed that it was cheaper to feed than to fight.

Any meeting had the potential of turning deadly. Sarah Royce looked up one day to see scores of mounted American Indians lining the trail. The men in

Gold seekers who followed the California Trail along the Humboldt River in Nevada often complained of losing livestock to Paiute raiders. Despite their skill with the bow and arrow, the Paiute could not stem the tide of settlement. In addition to their superior firepower, the settlers carried an invisible ally—deadly diseases such as measles and cholera.

the wagon train looked to their weapons, for an attack seemed certain. Instead, a chief stepped forward to offer safe passage in return for payment of a large toll. The Forty-Niners turned him down and signaled that they were ready to open fire. After a brief standoff, the American Indian warriors pulled back and allowed the wagons to roll past.[9]

A fair number of encounters did end in bloodshed. When emigrants caught cattle thieves in the act, they shot first and asked questions later. Both sides took casualties in these firefights. The Forty-Niners' rifles packed more punch, but a Paiute could fire a dozen arrows during the time it took his foes to reload. After a skirmish, the emigrants sometimes posted warnings along the trail:

> *Beware of Indians,*
> *They have shot several*
> *Animals & wounded a*
> *Man just below this.*[10]

Careful travelers drew their wagons together more closely and posted extra guards after reading one of these messages.

End of the Trail

The year 1850 marked a turning point in the history of the California Trail. In just three years, some fifty-seven thousand miners had crowded into the gold fields. Few saw their dreams of striking it rich come true. The rest labored and sweated and chased rumors from one "sure thing" to another. Each new diggings, they told themselves, would surely prove to be the fabled mother lode. One rumor sent miners hurrying north to the seacoast town of Trinidad. According to the story, the beach there was covered with "bright and yellow gold" at low tide. A slightly addled miner named Stoddard inspired another futile search. The goal this time was a mountain lake where he claimed to have seen nuggets scattered along the shore.[11] Both stories proved false.

As their money ran out, some miners gave up and went home. Those who stayed found jobs and built new lives in the fast-growing territory. On September 9,

SOURCE DOCUMENT

THE OLD-TIME SABBATH AMUSEMENTS OF RIDING BUCKING MUSTANGS INTO THE SALOONS, DRINKING ALL DAY AT THE VARIOUS BARS, RUNNING FOOT-RACES, PLAYING POKER, AND FINISHING THE DAY WITH A FREE FIGHT ARE THINGS OF THE PAST. THE SOBERING INFLUENCE OF CIVILIZATION HAS REMOVED ALL SUCH EXCITING BUT DANGEROUS PASTIMES AS PLAYING SCIENTIFIC GAMES OF BILLIARDS BY FIRING AT THE BALLS WITH A PISTOL, [AND] TAKING OFF THE HEADS OF THE DECANTERS [GLASSES USED FOR SERVING LIQUOR] BEHIND THE COUNTER WITH A QUICK SHOT. . . . NOW WHEN THE INDIVIDUAL MEMBERS OF THE ENLIGHTENED POPULATION PLAY CARDS, AS PERHAPS THEY SOMETIMES DO, IT IS IN THE SECLUSION OF THE BACK-ROOM, OUT OF RANGE OF PRYING EYES.[12]

California was a rough-and-ready man's world during the early days of the Gold Rush. That short-lived era faded when civilization caught up with the new state. Sunday gambling was first to go, outlawed in San Francisco in September 1850. Luzena Wilson, who wrote this report, rejoiced when the miners put a few more of their wild Sabbath sports to rest.

★ 95 ★

1850, Congress admitted California to the Union as the thirty-first state. When the news reached San Francisco on October 18, the city threw itself a party. People fired pistols into the air and danced around roaring bonfires.

Slowly, progress smoothed the rough edges of mining camp life. Ministers took over saloons for Sunday services and preached against liquor and gambling. Prodded by their wives, some miners signed a pledge to give up heavy drinking. Civic pride took root as secret lodges (the Masons and Odd Fellows, for example) raised money to help widows and orphans. Families moved in, and school boards went looking for teachers. Prentice Mulford won his teaching job by proving that he could spell words such as "cat" and "hat." A school board member gave Mulford a half-serious warning: "I wouldn't teach that school for $5,000 a year;" the man said. "There are two boys you'll have that I advise you to kill if possible the first week."[13]

With the gold fields playing out, the miners turned to other lines of work. Men and women with good heads for business long had prospered by "mining the miners." Now the marketplace looked even more promising. A young woman took in eleven thousand dollars selling pies she baked in a skillet. For a time, traders paid more to ship cargo from San Francisco to Sacramento than from New York to California. The steamship company that pioneered the routes made a fortune hauling goods and passengers on California's rivers. Alexander Todd and Levi Strauss became household names without touching a shovel. Todd built a thriving express service by picking up letters in San Francisco and delivering them to the gold fields. The mail-starved miners gladly paid him an ounce of gold dust per letter. Strauss became wealthy by selling a line of miner's jeans (later reinforced with copper rivets). The company he founded still sells Levi's around the globe.

Advances in transport and communication were bringing the era of the California Trail to a close. In 1855, the first train chugged over Panama's new cross-isthmus railroad. Compared to the overland route, a

Preachers and wives brought a classier lifestyle to California's rip-roaring mining towns. In this engraving, bearded miners raise a cheer as the town's first woman strolls along the unpaved street with her husband.

★ 97 ★

voyage to California via Panama now seemed quick and easy. The Butterfield Stage Line offered its own fast, bumpy ride via Santa Fe.

In 1860, William Russell and his partners pioneered a fast mail service across the west. Relays of Pony Express riders left St. Joseph, Missouri, and galloped into Sacramento ten days later. In just eighteen months, however, the completion of the east-west telegraph line ended the brief reign of the Pony Express.

For a time, emigrants too poor to travel by ship or by stage trickled westward along the old trails. The final blow to travel by wagon train fell in May 1869. Six years after the first rails were laid, the transcontinental railroad carried its first passengers. A journey across the United States would never be the same.

★ THE PONY EXPRESS: MARVEL OF AN AGE ★

In the late 1850s the Butterfield Overland Mail's southern route delivered mail to California in twenty-five days. William Russell, boss of a competing express company, yearned to beat Butterfield at its own game. He could cut the time in half, he figured, by following the California Trail's central route. The key, Russell told his partners, was to keep the mail moving. With that end in mind, they set up a chain of relay stations. Then they stocked their Overland Pony Express stations with hundreds of good horses.

The 1,966-mile route ran from St. Joseph, Missouri, to Sacramento, California. To do the riding, Russell advertised for eighty "young, skinny, wiry fellows, not over eighteen." Pony Express riders, the ad went on, must be "willing to risk death daily. Orphans preferred."[14] In the

Pony Express rider Frank Weber slowed down long enough to pose for this picture in 1861. Despite the heroic feats of riders like Weber, the Pony Express shut down after only eighteen months. The costly service could not compete with the telegraph.

early days, the riders covered stages of thirty to fifty miles. Later, longer stages of up to a hundred miles became the rule. Richard Egan once made his own run and then took a friend's run as a favor. The tireless Egan had ridden 330 miles by the time he made his final dismount.

The first Pony Express riders galloped out of Sacramento and St. Joseph on April 3, 1860. Ten days later the final riders in the relay chain delivered their precious pouches. Russell, deep in debt after building the relay stations, charged customers ten dollars an ounce. Later, even though he claimed it cost the Pony Express thirty-eight dollars to deliver a letter, the rate fell to two dollars an ounce.[15] Over a span of sixteen months, the daring riders made 308 runs in each direction. Despite daily brushes with danger, they lost only one shipment. That ill-fated rider died after he was ambushed by American Indians.

On October 24, 1861, the first east-west telegraph line crackled into life. The Pony Express, for all its glamour, could not match the speed of the new service. Russell and his partners had earned $101,000—and spent over a million. Two days later, with losses mounting, they ended the great experiment.

Buffalo Bill Cody, the great showman, refused to let the public forget Russell's great gamble. At age fourteen, young Billy Cody had galloped across Wyoming as a Pony Express rider. He remembered those stirring days when he organized his first Wild West Show in 1883.[16] The thrilling sight of Pony Express riders thundering around the arenas at breakneck speed brought roars of approval from Cody's fans.

8

THE CALIFORNIA TRAIL TODAY

L ydia Waters and her husband followed the California Trail westward in 1855. Her account of the long trek describes bad days and good days in the same quiet voice. The party had "fine times" in the Mohawk Valley, Lydia noted, "although [we were] surrounded by grizzly bears and large wolves." After she reached Sacramento, she jotted down a final matter-of-fact entry. "For six months and three days we had lived in our wagons and traveled many a weary mile," Lydia wrote. "Many a laughable incident comes to my mind which would make this account too lengthy."[1]

Today, the California Trail has given way to high-speed roads such as Interstate 80 and U.S. Highway 50. A modern Waters family can jump into the minivan and retrace Lydia Waters's trip in a matter of days. If the travelers are typical, they will scarcely notice the countryside. The kids will nag, "How many more miles to Disneyland?" Instead of worrying about finding a spring, the parents will worry about finding a motel with a swimming pool.

Americans who appreciate the California Trail's role in history move to a different drumbeat. Their rule is, "Slow down! Your country's past is calling to you." A look at a good guidebook shows that traces of the old trails lie waiting to be explored. Museums, parks, old buildings, and natural landmarks all have tales to tell. Although the last wagons rolled past around 1890, the California Trail lives on.

Walk in the Footsteps of the Forty-Niners

Tourists drive over and past the same landmarks that marked the route our ancestors followed. The Platte, Sweetwater, and Humboldt Rivers still flow. Chimney Rock still points its spire skyward. Down at ground level, bulldozers and plows have erased most of the ruts left by thousands of overloaded wagons. The routes chosen by today's roadbuilders, however, sometimes veer away from the old trail. As George Stewart writes in *The California Trail*, "In such still-undeveloped areas the traces of the trail can often be discerned for many miles."[2]

What clues tell trail-seekers that they are on the right track? Match a trail map to a map of the modern towns and highways that sprawl across its route. The overlay will spotlight the trail's surviving landmarks, forts, trading posts, and stopping points. Members of the Oregon-California Trails Association (OCTA) and other groups have done exactly that. These trail buffs have searched out, marked, and preserved traces that might well have been lost.

By 1912, the glory days of the California Trail were fading. This photo, taken near Big Springs, Nebraska, captured a moment in time when the past and the future came face-to-face.

At Deep Rut Hill, near Guernsey, Wyoming, wagons carved deep grooves into the rocks. The names carved and painted on the same state's Register Cliff and Independence Rock prove that graffiti is not a modern invention. On the west slope of the Sierras, boulders display scrape marks left by the passage of iron wheels. In Nevada, the Forty-Mile Desert hides a treasure trove of "trash" dropped by the settlers. Robert Laxalt found rusted barrel hoops, shards of pottery, bits of glass, and an abundance of sun-bleached bones.[3]

Laxalt also wandered along the twisting path of the Humboldt River. After turning off Interstate 80 he parked his jeep and trudged into the sagebrush desert. "As I walked I tried to imagine the sufferings of the pioneers," he writes. "The vast dome of the sky was a hot, burning blue, the sun a relentless, blinding orb. There was not a tree anywhere, and I imagined the yearning of the pioneers for one tiny bit of shade. The shimmering desert seemed to suck the moisture out of my body. In the afternoon a breeze sprang up, but . . . the eddies of air were like gusts from a blast furnace. I began to imagine the pioneers' state of mind as they realized that the worst was yet to come."[4]

Laxalt later met a modern Forty-Niner along the trail. Barbara Maat, a young Massachusetts woman, was retracing the route—on foot. "I was fascinated and awed by the pioneers' walking across the country. I could hardly believe it," she explained. Following in the footsteps of the Donner party, Maat walked from Missouri to Sacramento. Reality struck home the night snow fell while she was nestled in a sleeping bag at Donner Lake. "I cried when I woke up to see the snow," she said. "I was overwhelmed when I imagined their misery and terror."[5]

A Travel Plan for Trail Seekers

Only the most heroic trail buffs attempt to retrace the California Trail on foot. For the most part, tourists are content to consult guidebooks and seek out appealing segments of the old trail. Here are some choice places to visit (traveling east to west):

Independence and St. Joseph, Missouri.

The Forty-Niners knew these Missouri towns as jumping off points for the trails west. Independence houses the National Frontier Trails Center, where displays tell the story of the town's role as the hub of the Santa Fe, California, and Oregon Trails. On Labor Day weekend, Independence kicks up its heels at Santa-Cali-Gon Days. The festival features costumed "pioneers," Old West shootouts, carnival rides, and down-home bluegrass music. In St. Joseph, the Pony Express Stables Museum beckons tourists. The exhibits are housed in the stables that once served as the eastern end of the famed mail service.

Fort Kearny

Army forts guarded key points along the trail. After the long trek across Nebraska, Fort Kearny and the nearby Platte River were welcome sights. The river was "too thick to drink, too thin to plow," but the fort meant safety and a chance to replace sickly oxen. Today's visitors wander through the old fort, which has been rebuilt as the centerpiece of a historic park. A stroll across the parade grounds brings the words of Lucena Parsons to life. On July 4, 1850, she wrote, "We were in hearing of cannon at old Fort Carny & it seemed like home. We are all on the river bank & in sight of each other."[6]

Courthouse Rock and Chimney Rock

Almost every emigrant who kept a journal or diary mentions these landmarks. Wind and rain have shaped the contours of massive Courthouse Rock, which lies some six miles from Bridgeport, Nebraska. When the wind comes up at night campers claim to hear the sound of ghostly singing from atop the rock. Legend says the sound is made by the spirits of dead Pawnee warriors. Chimney Rock, by contrast, is a slender stone spire that juts up from a large cone. The "chimney" looks majestic, even though natural forces have

One way to recapture the spirit of life on the California Trail is to travel with a modern wagon train. Here, the nearly unspoiled wilderness of Nebraska's Wildcat Hills dwarfs a party of trekkers and their wagons.

whittled away at least fifty feet from its height since the 1850s. As was their custom, emigrants paused here to carve their names in the soft sandstone.

Platte River Crossing and Fort Caspar

Near Caspar, Wyoming, trail-seekers can relive the challenge of crossing the North Platte River. The Mormon ferry operated here from 1847 to 1851. The sight of wagons lined up for the ferry inspired John Richard to build a bridge across the Platte. His first bridge was a great success—until spring floods washed it away in 1852. A replica of the ferry and a sturdy log bridge that dates back to 1858 attract tourists to Fort Caspar. The Interpretive Center's exhibits tell the story of American Indians, soldiers, settlers, and prospectors.

Independence Rock

For the Forty-Niners, the rounded mass of Independence Rock marked the approach to the Sweetwater River. The thousands of names cut and painted on the great granite rock led a pioneer priest to dub it "the Great Register of the Desert."[7] Experts say that "registering" a name told those who came later that a friend had passed that way. James Nesmith described his own visit in 1843. "After breakfast, . . . I had the satisfaction of putting the names of Miss Mary Zachary and Miss Jane Mills on the southeast point of the rock," he wrote. "Facing the road, in all splendor of gun powder, tar, and buffalo grease, may be seen the name of J. W. Nesmith, from Maine, with an anchor."[8]

South Pass

The ascent to Wyoming's South Pass told settlers that they were nearing the Continental Divide. The Continental Divide is the point at which the rivers begin to flow west instead of east. Soon emigrants bound for California would bid farewell to their friends headed for Oregon. The pass itself was not nearly as steep as Windlass Hill in Nebraska, which one man described as hanging "a little past the perpendicular!"[9] Here at South Pass, with snow-capped peaks looming nearby, the climb was gradual. North of the paved road, hikers walk past old stone markers along a trail "worn down beneath the general level of the ground."[10] OCTA has campaigned to win a listing for South Pass in the National Register of Historic Places. Doing so, members say, will keep the site from being spoiled by further development.

Mormon Station

The long haul across the Forty-Mile Desert brought the emigrants to the Mormon Station trading post. Located in the Carson Valley, the tiny town (later renamed Genoa) survived to become Nevada's first permanent settlement. In the 1850s, business was brisk at the station's store, blacksmith shop, flour mill, and sawmill. A guidebook warned, "We would advise all to stop in the valley and recruit [rest] their teams before crossing the Nevada mountains."[11] The state turned the site into a historic park in 1947.

A guide leads a team of modern trekkers toward Courthouse Rock, a well-known landmark on the old California Trail. At night, campers sometimes claim to hear the sound of dead Pawnee warriors singing from atop the massive monument.

Carson River Route

From the Carson Valley, wagon trains passed through Carson Canyon before tackling the Sierra Nevada. Ahead lay 8,600-foot Carson Pass and 9,600-foot West Pass. Despite the hard going, this was said to be the easiest route to the gold fields. Today's travelers cruise the same route on U.S. Highway 50. At Carson Pass, they pile out of their cars to enjoy the breathtaking view. A short walk takes them to a spot where traces of the old trail can be seen. Emigrants carved their names into the rocks, marked a grave, and left wheel ruts etched into the hillside.

Marshall Gold Discovery State Historic Park and Sutter's Fort, California

Trailseekers turn off U.S. Highway 50 at historic Placerville and follow State Route 49 to quiet little Coloma. Here, on the American River, they can stand on the spot where James Marshall kicked off the Gold Rush. Waiting a few yards away are the rebuilt sawmill and a small Gold Rush museum. To visit Sutter's Fort, tourists take U.S. Highway 50 into the heart of Sacramento. The reconstructed fort and its Gold Rush displays have been preserved at Twentieth and L Streets. Not far away is Old Sacramento, where Gold Rush-era buildings, shops, and museums keep the past alive.

★ IT IS NOT TOO LATE TO GO TRAIL-SEEKING ★

How would you like to travel the California Trail? That is not as crazy as it sounds. A growing number of Americans are doing exactly that. If you have access to the Internet, you can take a virtual trip to California. Better yet, your family can arrange to travel with a wagon train. And if you are really bitten by the trail bug, you can join a group that recreates the life and times of the early settlers.

To take the trek by computer, turn your browser to:

http://www.OCTA-trails.org

The Oregon-California Trail Association (OCTA) sponsors this well-designed web site. After a brief foreword, the screen invites you to jump off from Independence or St. Joseph. If you choose St. Joseph, the next screen takes you to the Iowa, Sac and Fox Mission, two days' journey along the trail. Like the other stops along the way, this screen offers a history of the site, complete with photos. Next, click 'Continue on the Trail' and you'll jump to Hollenberg Stage Station. A third click takes you on to Fort Kearny. Screen by screen, the trail leads on to Stop 25—the end of the trail at Sutter's Fort. "Congratulations!" OCTA says. "You have successfully completed your trek across the California Trail. We hope you find great prosperity in your new home."[12]

Several outfits give greenhorns a chance to get a first-hand feel for the trail. One is Oregon Trail Wagon Train (Route 2, Box 200B, Bayard, Nebraska 69334). Another is Historic Trails Expeditions (PO Box 428, Mills, Wyoming

Andrew Green relived pioneer days when he journeyed westward with the Oregon Trail Wagon Train. Here he relaxes with several four-footed friends during an afternoon break. In the days that followed, Green and the other trail trekkers drove the wagons, fired muzzle-loading rifles, and cooked their meals over open fires.

SOURCE DOCUMENT

THE HUMBUG

FROM ALL THE BOOKS THAT WE HAVE READ
AND ALL THE TRAVELERS HAVE SAID
WE MOST IMPLICITLY BELIEVED,
NOT DREAMED THAT WE SHOULD BE DECEIVED

THAT WHEN THE MOUNTAINS WE SHOULD PASS
WE'D FIND ON HUMBOLDT FINE BLUE GRASS.
NAY THAT'S NOT ALL, WE LEARNED MOREOVER
THAT WE'D GET IN THE MIDST OF CLOVER. . . .

BUT WHEN WE TO THE HUMBOLDT CAME
IT SOON WITH US LOST ALL ITS FAME;
WE VIEWED IT AS A GREAT OUTRAGE
INSTEAD OF GRASS TO FIND WILD SAGE.[13]

Today's trail-seekers tend to agree with the emigrants who learned to detest the Humboldt River. The sluggish stream winds through 365 miles of rocks, heat, and prickly pear. To make matters worse, the water turns alkaline and grass gives way to sagebrush as the river nears the Humboldt Sink. So join the weary travelers as they sing about the river they nicknamed the Humbug.

82644). The guides give everyone a chance to take an active role. "Emigrants" drive covered wagons, fire muzzle-loading rifles, cook over open fires, and ride horseback. As a bonus, the Oregon Trail Wagon Train takes you on tours of Independence Rock and Chimney Rock. Although the four-day trip costs around $125 a day for adults and $95 a day for children, the experience may well be priceless.

Hard core trail-seekers dress, hunt, eat, and travel like the early pioneers. People taking part in historical reenactments put on trail garb and gather at a rendezvous point each year to celebrate trail history. Historical Trekkers spend as much time out on the trail as they can. Their goal is to live an authentic frontier life during their stays in the wilderness. Information about Reenactments and Trekkers can be found in *On the Trail* magazine (PO Box 276, Sumiton, Alabama 35148).

★ TIMELINE ★

1542—Juan Rodríquez Cabrillo explores the California coast and claims the land for Spain. England's Sir Francis Drake sails along the same coastline in 1579.

1760s—Russian traders hunt seals and otters along the northern California coast.

1767—The Spanish send settlers to California and Father Junípero Serra's era of mission building begins.

1819—The United States and Spain establish the northern boundary of Mexico at the forty-second parallel. Russia retains its outpost at Fort Ross.

1825—Four years after Mexico wins independence, California becomes a territory of the new republic. American ships trade with the rancheros for hides, tallow, and sea otter pelts.

1826—Jedediah Smith leads a party from Utah to the San Gabriel mission near Los Angeles. The great mountain man forges a key link in the California Trail when he heads directly across the Sierra Nevada on his return trip.

1827—Independence, Missouri, is founded. The town later prospers as the jumping-off place for the Santa Fe and Oregon-California Trails.

1833 -1834—Mountain man Joseph Walker opens a route across the Sierra Nevada that will become part of the California Trail.

1839—John Sutter obtains several California land grants. His headquarters at Sutter's Fort later becomes a magnet for newcomers. In 1841, he buys Fort Ross from the Russians, who abandon their interests in the territory.

1841—The Bartleson-Bidwell party makes history by becoming the first emigrant group to cross the Sierra Nevada.

1842—Kit Carson guides John C. Frémont across South Pass and the Rocky Mountains. Later emigrants depend heavily on Frémont's maps.

1844—Elisha Stephens and his party take the first wagons over the Sierra Nevada.

1846 -1847—The Donner party meets disaster after being snowed in near Donner Lake.

1846 -1848—The Bear Flag Revolt ends Mexican rule in California, but the new flag soon gives way to the Stars and Stripes. The Mexican War drags to a close in 1848. The United States gains what is now California, Arizona, New Mexico, Nevada, and Utah.

1848—James Marshall finds gold in a millrace on the American River. The news spreads quickly, triggering the California Gold Rush.

1849—Gold seekers pour into California by land and sea. Wagon trains probe for cutoffs along the torturous trail, but with little success.

1850—California enters the Union as a free state, meaning that it forbid slavery.

1852—Over fifty thousand emigrants, many with their families, hurry toward the Golden State. Thanks to improved conditions along the trail, wagons that took 136 days to make the trip in 1846 now reach California in as little as seventy-six days.

1857—Congress spends $300,000 for further improvements to the trail.

1859—The newly opened Lander Road cuts down on desert travel, much to the relief of new emigrants.

1860—Pony Express riders deliver mail from Missouri to Sacramento in only ten days. The colorful service ends with the completion of the first telegraph line in 1861.

1869—The opening of the transcontinental railroad signals the beginning of the end for the California Trail.

★ CHAPTER NOTES ★

Chapter 1. The Golden Lure

1. William Weber Johnson, *The Forty-Niners* (New York: Time-Life Books, 1974), p. 43.

2. J. S. Holliday, *The World Rushed In: The California Gold Rush Experience* (New York: Simon & Schuster, 1981), p. 33.

3. Johnson, p. 33.

4. Ibid., p. 17.

5. Holliday, p. 48.

6. Frederick Jackson Turner, *The Significance of the Frontier in American History* (New York: Frederick Ungar Publishing Co., 1963), p. 28.

Chapter 2. An Island Called California

1. Michael Kowalewski, ed., *Gold Rush: A Literary Exposition* (Berkeley, Calif.: Heyday Books, 1997), p. 5.

2. Warren A. Beck and David A. Williams, *California: A History of the Golden State* (Garden City, NY: Doubleday & Co., 1972), p. 81.

3. Richard Henry Dana, *Two Years Before the Mast* (New York: The Modern Library, 1936), p. 79.

4. Beck and Williams, p. 90.

5. Kowalewski, p. 33.

6. Dana, pp. 253–257.

Chapter 3. Gold Fever Strikes

1. Rodman W. Paul, *California Gold: The Beginning of Mining in the Far West* (Lincoln: University of Nebraska Press, 1947), pp. 18–19.

2. William Weber Johnson, *The Forty-Niners* (New York: Time-Life Books, 1974), p. 19.

3. Ibid., p. 38.

4. Paul, p. 30.

5. Michael Kowalewski, ed., *Gold Rush: A Literary Exposition* (Berkeley, Calif.: Heyday Books, 1997), p. 36.

6. J. S. Holliday, *The World Rushed In: The California Gold Rush Experience* (New York: Simon & Schuster, 1981), p. 62.

7. Peter Browning, ed., *To the Golden Shore: America Goes to California—1849* (Lafayette, Calif.: Great West Books, 1995), pp. 80, 87.

8. Johnson, pp. 46–47.

9. Holliday, pp. 62, 138.

10. Paul, p. 32.

11. Kowalewski, pp. 119–120.

12. Paul, p. 34.

13. Joseph Henry Jackson, *Anybody's Gold: The Story of California's Mining Towns* (San Francisco: Chronicle Books, 1970), pp. 50–53.

Chapter 4. The Long Way Around

1. Peter Browning, ed., *To the Golden Shore: America Goes to California—1849* (Lafayette, Calif.: Great West Books, 1995), p. 78.

2. William Weber Johnson, *The Forty-Niners* (New York: Time-Life Books, 1974), p. 52.

3. Browning, pp. 118–119.

4. Joann Levy, *They Saw the Elephant: Women in the California Gold Rush* (Hamden, Conn.: Archon Books, 1990), p. 37.

5. Michael Kowalewski, ed., *Gold Rush; A Literary Exposition* (Berkeley, Calif.: Heyday Books, 1997), p. 63.

6. Joseph Henry Jackson, *Anybody's Gold: The Story of California's Mining Towns* (San Francisco: Chronicle Books, 1970), p. 34.

7. Richard Henry Dana, *Two Years Before the Mast* (New York: The Modern Library, 1936), p. 52.

8. Levy, p. 31.

9. Ibid., pp. 31–32.

10. Peter Browning, ed., *To the Golden Shore; America Goes to California—1849* (Lafayette, Calif.: Great West Books, 1995), pp. 133–134.

11. Levy, p. 38.

12. Ibid., p. 41.

13. Browning, p. 407.

14. Ibid., p. 405.

15. Kowalewski, p. 65.

16. Warren A. Beck and David A. Williams, *California: A History of the Golden State* (Garden City, NY: Doubleday & Co., 1972), p. 198.

Chapter 5. Looking for the Elephant

1. Joann Levy, *They Saw the Elephant: Women in the California Gold Rush* (Hamden, Conn.: Archon Books, 1990), p. xvi.

2. Ibid., p. 1.

3. Peter Browning, ed., *To the Golden Shore: America Goes to California—1849* (Lafayette, Calif.: Great West Books, 1995), p. 240.

4. Joseph Henry Jackson, *Anybody's Gold: The Story of California's Mining Towns* (San Francisco: Chronicle Books, 1970), p. 39.

5. William Weber Johnson, *The Forty-Niners* (New York: Time-Life Books, 1974), p. 61.

6. William E. Hill, *The California Trail: Yesterday & Today* (Boise, Idaho: Tamarack Books, 1993), p. 36.

7. Ibid., pp. 36–38.

8. Sarah Royce, *A Frontier Lady: Recollections of the Gold Rush and Early California* (Lincoln: University of Nebraska Press, 1977), p. 72.

9. Browning, p. 207.

10. George R. Stewart, *The California Trail: An Epic with Many Heroes* (Lincoln: University of Nebraska Press, 1962), pp. 118–119.

11. Ibid., p. 229.

12. Ibid., p. 118.

13. Lew Smith, *The American Dream* (Glenview, Ill.: Scott, Foresman & Co., 1980), p. 208.

14. Johnson, p. 58.

15. Hill, pp. 45–48.

16. Adapted from Stewart, p. 113.

17. Stewart, pp. 113–114.

Chapter 6. "The Road was Lined with Skeletons"

1. George R. Stewart, *The California Trail: An Epic with Many Heroes* (Lincoln: University of Nebraska Press, 1962), p. 146.

2. Joann Levy, *They Saw the Elephant: Women in the California Gold Rush* (Hamden, Conn.: Archon Books, 1990), p. 24.

3. Irwin Silber, ed., *Songs of the Great American West* (New York: Dover Publications, 1995), p. 10.

4. Peter Browning, ed., *To the Golden Shore: America Goes to California—1849* (Lafayette, Calif.: Great West Books, 1995), p. 403.

5. Stewart, p. 266.

6. J. S. Holliday, *The World Rushed In: the California Gold Rush Experience* (New York: Simon & Schuster, 1981), p. 178.

7. Lew Smith, *The American Dream* (Glenview, Ill.: Scott, Foresman and Co., 1980), p. 211.

8. Levy, p. 18.

9. Stewart, pp. 326–327.

10. Holliday, pp. 285–286.

11. Ibid., pp. 192–193.

12. Sarah Royce, *A Frontier Lady: Recollections of the Gold Rush and Early California* (Lincoln: University of Nebraska Press, 1977), pp. 16–17.

13. Smith, p. 210.

14. Stewart, p. 154.

15. Holliday, p. 189.

16. Ibid., p. 229.

17. Browning, p. 403.

18. Robert Kirsch and William S. Murphy, *West of the West* (New York: E. P. Dutton & Co., 1967), p. 287.

19. National Geographic Society, *Trails West* (Washington, D.C.: National Geographic Society, 1979), p. 136.

Chapter 7. The Trail Prospers . . . And Dies

1. J. S. Holliday, *The World Rushed In: The California Gold Rush Experience* (New York: Simon and Schuster, 1981), p. 290.

2. Peter H. Burnett, *An Old California Pioneer* (Oakland, Calif.: Biobooks, 1946), p. 164.

3. William E. Hill, *The California Trail: Yesterday & Today* (Boise, Idaho: Tamarack Books, 1993), pp. 26–28.

4. George R. Stewart, *The California Trail: An Epic with Many Heroes* (Lincoln: University of Nebraska Press, 1962), pp. 297–299.

5. Joann Levy, *They Saw the Elephant: Women in the California Gold Rush* (Hamden, Conn.: Archon Books, 1990), p. xvi.

6. Holliday, p. 114.

7. Dee Brown, *Wondrous Times on the Frontier* (New York: Harper Perennial, 1991), pp. 188–189.

8. Holliday, pp. 241–242.

9. Sarah Royce, *A Frontier Lady: Recollections of the Gold Rush and Early California* (Lincoln: University of Nebraska Press, 1977), pp. 13–14.

10. Stewart, p. 276.

11. Joseph Henry Jackson, *Anybody's Gold: The Story of California's Mining Towns* (San Francisco: Chronicle Books, 1970), pp. 64–66.

12. Levy, p. 205.

13. William Weber Johnson, *The Forty-Niners* (New York: Time-Life Books, 1974), p. 140.

14. National Geographic Society, *Trails West* (Washington, D.C.: National Geographic Society, 1979), p. 127.

15. Warren A. Beck and David A. Williams, *California: A History of the Golden State* (Garden City, N.Y.: Doubleday & Co., 1972), p. 206.

16. Gorton Carruth and Associates, *The Encyclopedia of American Facts and Dates* (New York: Thomas Crowell, 1970), p. 329.

Chapter 8. The California Trail Today

1. Lew Smith, *The American Dream* (Glenview, Ill.: Scott, Foresman & Co., 1980), p. 211.

2. George R. Stewart, *The California Trail: An Epic with Many Heroes* (Lincoln: University of Nebraska Press, 1962), p. 320.

3. National Geographic Society, *Trails West* (Washington, D.C.: National Geographic Society, 1979), p. 120.

4. Ibid., p. 112.

5. Ibid., pp. 114–115, 137.

6. Oregon-California Trails Association, "Fort Kearny," OCTA Virtual Tour. n.d. <http://calcite.rocky.edu/octa/ftk.htm> (February 1, 2000).

7. William E. Hill, *The California Trail: Yesterday & Today* (Boise, Idaho: Tamarack Books, 1993), p. 129.

8. Robert L. Munkres and Richard Klein, "Independence Rock," OCTA Virtual Tour. n.d. <http://calcite.rocky.edu/octa/ir.htm> (February 1, 2000).

9. *Trails West*, p. 59.

10. Stewart, p. 320.

11. Oregon-California Trails Association, "Mormon Station," OCTA Virtual Tour. n.d. <http://calcite.rocky.edu/octa/morsta.htm> (February 1, 2000).

12. Oregon-California Trails Association, "California Trail Virtual Tour," OCTA Virtual Tour. n.d. <http://calcite.rocky.edu/octa/trailmap.htm> (February 1, 2000).

13. Hill, p. 190.

★ FURTHER READING ★

Blumberg, Rhoda. *The Great American Gold Rush*. New York: Bradbury Press, 1989.

Browning, Peter, ed. *To the Golden Shore: America Goes to California—1849*. Lafayette, Calif.: Great West Books, 1995.

Bullard, William C. *Bound for the Promised Land*. Independence, Mo.: The National Frontier Trails Center, 1990.

Clark, Thomas D., ed. *Gold Rush Diary; Being the Journal of Elisha Douglass Perkins on the Overland Trail in the Spring and Summer of 1849*. Lexington: University of Kentucky Press, 1967.

Hill, William E. *The California Trail, Yesterday and Today*. Boise, Idaho: Tamarack Books, Inc., 1993.

Holliday, J. S. *The World Rushed In: The California Gold Rush Experience*. New York: Simon & Schuster, 1981.

Hulbert, Archer Butler. *Forty-Niners: The Chronicle of the California Trail*. Las Vegas, Nev.: Nevada Publications, 1986. (Originally published 1931.)

Jackson, Joseph Henry. *Anybody's Gold: The Story of California's Mining Towns*. San Francisco: Chronicle Books, 1970.

Johnson, William Weber. *The Forty-Niners*. New York: Time-Life Books, 1974.

Ketchum, Liza. *The Gold Rush*. Boston: Little, Brown and Co., 1996.

Kowalewski, Michael, ed. *Gold Rush: A Literary Exposition*. Berkeley, Calif.: Heyday Books, 1997.

Krisch, Robert, and William S. Murphy. *West of the West*. New York: E. P. Dutton & Co., 1967.

Levy, Joann. *They Saw the Elephant: Women in the California Gold Rush*. Hamden, Conn.: Archon Books, 1990.

National Geographic Society. *Trails West*. Washington, D.C.: National Geographic Society, 1979.

Paul, Rodman W. *California Gold: The Beginning of Mining in the Far West*. Lincoln: University of Nebraska Press, 1947.

Peters, Arthur King. *Seven Trails West*. New York: Abbeville Press, 1996.

Royce, Sarah. *A Frontier Lady: Recollections of the Gold Rush and Early California*. Lincoln: University of Nebraska Press, 1977. (Reprint of 1932 edition.)

Sanford, William R., and Carl R. Green. *John C. Frémont: Soldier and Pathfinder*. Springfield, N.J.: Enslow Publishers, 1996.

Stefoff, Rebecca. *The Oregon Trail in American History*. Springfield, N.J.: Enslow Publishers, 1997.

Stewart, George R. *The California Trail: An Epic with Many Heroes*. Lincoln: University of Nebraska Press, 1962.

Internet Addresses

Fox, Lawrence. *The Museum of Sutter's Fort*. n.d. <http://score.rims.d12.ca.us/activity/suttersfort/sutters_fort.html> (February 16, 2000).

Historic Trails West. *The "Official California Trail Gold Rush Wagon Train of the 49'rs."* February 1, 2000. <http://www.goldrushwagontrain.com> (February 16, 2000).

The Donner Party. n.d. <http://www.tahoenet.com/tdhs/tpdonner.html> (February 16, 2000).

The National Oregon/California Trail Center at Clover Creek in Montpelier, Idaho. January 11, 2000. <http://www.oregontrailcenter.org> (February 16, 2000).

Wischmann, Lesley. *Oregon-California Trails Association*. January 21, 2000. <http://www.OCTA-trails.org> (February 16, 2000).

★ INDEX ★